Small Business Accounting

Small Business Accounting

Andy Lymer

First published in Great Britain in 2010 by Hodder Headline. An Hachette UK company.

This edition published in 2015 by John Murray Learning

British Library Cataloguing in Publication Data: a catalogue record for this title is available from the British Library.

ISBN 9781473609174

eISBN 9781473623729

1

The publisher has used its best endeavours to ensure that any website addresses referred to in this book are correct and active at the time of going to press. However, the publisher and the author have no responsibility for the websites and can make no guarantee that a site will remain live or that the content will remain relevant, decent or appropriate.

The publisher has made every effort to mark as such all words which it believes to be trademarks. The publisher should also like to make it clear that the presence of a word in the book, whether marked or unmarked, in no way affects its legal status as a trademark.

Every reasonable effort has been made by the publisher to trace the copyright holders of material in this book. Any errors or omissions should be notified in writing to the publisher, who will endeavour to rectify the situation for any reprints and future editions.

Cover image © Shutterstock.com

Typeset by Cenveo® Publisher Services.

Printed and bound in Great Britain by CPI Group (UK) Ltd., Croydon, CR0 4YY.

John Murray Learning policy is to use papers that are natural, renewable and recyclable products and made from wood grown in sustainable forests. The logging and manufacturing processes are expected to conform to the environmental regulations of the country of origin.

Carmelite House
50 Victoria Embankment
London EC4Y 0DZ
www.hodder.co.uk

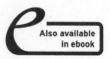

Contents

Meet the author

This book is intended for the small business owner with no knowledge of – or detailed interest in – book-keeping and accountancy. The simple book-keeping system explained here is for real businesses that need a straightforward, understandable and reliable system for record-keeping. It can be used by the smallest of businesses, operating as part-time as well as full-time ventures, and by those who have no aptitude for figures. Provided you can more or less understand what a bank statement means, you can understand the record-keeping system outlined in this book.

The system does not assume that you know anything at all about business records and accounts, and the book uses practical examples of real businesses (a building business, a village shop and a taxi driver) to show, step by step, how to record typical business transactions. The system will ensure that you can produce a complete and correct set of books for your business.

This book was originally written by Mike Truman and J. Randall Stott and updated in recent editions by David Lloyd; I gratefully acknowledge the foundation work done by these prior authors on whose significant efforts I have tried to build further as part of the development and updating of this title for this edition.

I hope you enjoy the book and gain in business confidence as a direct result.

Andy Lymer, 2015

Introduction

In this chapter you will learn:

- ▶ *Who this book is aimed at*
- ▶ *Why this book is different*
- ▶ *How to use this book*

Who this book is aimed at

Many qualified accountants will recommend a similar system to the one discussed in this book when advising smaller business clients. Unfortunately however, accountants do not always have time to explain the method in great detail. This book fills that gap. The system is based around business bank statements, from which the figures are then analysed into various categories of income and expenditure. The method is what is referred to as single entry, with each business transaction being entered in the records only once.

The system requires nothing more than pencil and paper, although it does lend itself readily to being set up using a computerized spreadsheet program, eliminating much of the manual work involved in using a calculator to add up columns of figures. Some basic tips on how to set up a spreadsheet are included.

As well as providing a tried and tested method to handle real business book-keeping, this book also demonstrates, using worked examples, how to keep business financial paperwork. It even provides some guidance for completing your annual tax return.

The system will not be suitable for businesses that need to maintain records for large numbers of customers or suppliers who are trading on credit terms. However, the method has been used by many hundreds of thousands of businesses over the years and, by incorporating appropriate enhancements as they grew in size and complexity, many did not need to relinquish it until they became very much larger. Indeed, size isn't the key issue in switching from this system – complexity is, as the more complex the business becomes, the more need there is for a full accounting system.

The system is ideal for the majority of smaller businesses that operate with just one bank account, but where more than one account exists, separate books can be run for each so this system will continue to apply. The system will cope with straightforward loan financing arrangements, although it does so in an unorthodox way in order to avoid getting too far into accounting jargon.

This book is intended primarily for sole traders, people who own and run their business personally. It is also suitable for use by husband-and-wife type partnerships, where there is no need to split monies taken out ('drawings') between the two partners. Such partnerships should treat all references to 'the proprietor' as references to the partners. The information on completing the annual tax return will apply equally to the partnership tax return, but more complex partnerships should take professional advice on the adaptations needed to this system for their purposes, as will anyone running their business as a limited company, as different accounting rules apply for companies. The book also provides guidance on how to choose an accountant.

If you already use a computerized accounting package, the method of entering accounting transactions will be different from the manual system set out here. However, the information about filing and cross-checking from invoices will still apply, as will the information about completing your annual tax return. If the computer package you already use is one that is based around the business bank account then you will find a number of similarities between the way it operates and this system, since both handle data in much the same way. The computer simply hides the method of analysis from view. Simple Cloud-based accounting systems do likewise if you opt for such a solution.

Using this book in conjunction with the manual supplied with an accounting package or an online guide may, therefore, help you work out how to enter more unusual accounting transactions.

Case studies

It is much easier to understand any system when you can see it in use. Books teaching a book-keeping system can sometimes use examples that are unconnected, and readers therefore see no picture of how the system builds up gradually. This is adequate if you are learning about accounting to pass exams but is not as helpful if you are learning because you need to do accounting for a real business. Additionally, examples are only from manufacturing businesses, whereas most small businesses in the UK are in the retail or service sectors.

So that you can see the system in operation three different case studies are used in this book. Ben Martin is a self-employed taxi driver, Grace Morris runs a village shop, and Hardip Singh is a builder. Background information for the case studies is given below.

Not all the case studies appear in each chapter. Sometimes one is used to illustrate particular problems or unusual transactions arising in that broad type of business, and which need to be recorded in a particular way. At other times one business is followed through several chapters so that you can become familiar with the transactions being recorded.

When you are reading through the book, please follow the examples fully. It may be tempting to skip over the detailed figures and go into the explanations, but the way to get the most out of the examples is to follow them line by line and to understand each one fully before moving on.

HARDIP SINGH – BUILDER

Hardip Singh is a builder. He occasionally works as a subcontractor for other builders, but normally works directly for clients, carrying out small building maintenance jobs. He has no permanent staff, but employs casual labourers from time to time. As their employer, he must account for income tax under the PAYE ('Pay As You Earn') system on their wages.

Mr Singh's office is a table in his home, where he writes up his business records, and where his van and tools are kept overnight. His partner acts as a part-time secretary for him, taking messages and making telephone calls. He works on invoice, giving his customers a bill which they pay later. Sometimes he is paid immediately, either in cash or by cheque. He has a trade account with a local builders' merchant where he buys most of his building materials, but he also goes to DIY stores where he pays for materials by cheque or by credit card.

GRACE MORRIS – SHOPKEEPER

Grace Morris runs a village shop, selling food, sweets and newspapers. The shop is rented, and she and her husband live in the flat upstairs. Mrs Morris's customers pay her as they purchase goods, in cash or by debit or credit card. The exception is newspaper deliveries, for which people come into the shop and settle their bills once every two weeks or so.

Purchases are made partly from a large Cash and Carry store, where she uses a business credit card, and partly from wholesalers who invoice her. Newspapers and magazines come from a wholesale newsagent. She employs three teenagers to deliver the newspapers, and some part-time help in the shop.

BEN MARTIN – TAXI DRIVER

Ben Martin is a taxi driver. He works partly by picking up fares who hail him on the street, and partly by bookings made through another company, Cab-U-Like, which provides him with a two-way radio. He is almost always paid in cash by the customers he picks up from the street. However, when he takes a Cab-U-Like client he is not paid directly, but receives a bank transfer from Cab-U-Like in the first week of each month for the fares he carried during the previous month. Mr Martin's major running expenses are usually paid by credit card or by cheque, and he pays in cash for minor expenses.

Why this book is different and how to use it

If you have looked at other books on accountancy and book-keeping before buying this one, you will know that they are generally full of accounting jargon. They refer to ledgers and journals and 'double-entry' accounting, and you sometimes feel you need a dictionary by your side to read them. Do you really need to know all of this to handle the finances of a small business? No, of course you don't. Most of these books are not aimed primarily at owners of small businesses, they are written for students taking courses in book-keeping and accounts or set out a version of book-keeping better suited to much larger businesses.

That system, so-called double-entry accounting, has been around for more than five centuries, and can be used to produce accounts for anything from a small business to an international company. It automatically includes an internal cross-checking process to minimize the risk of errors remaining undetected. It can be very complicated to learn and, as the name suggests, involves writing up each transaction twice, once as a 'debit' entry and once as a 'credit' entry. However, for many smaller businesses there is often no need to run a double-entry system if you don't want to.

The system described in this book enters accounting transactions using a single entry, and the series of case studies will guide you and also show you how to cope with some quite complex transactions.

At the end of your business year, you have a choice. If you choose to pay for an accountant to deal with your tax affairs, you can present him or her with a complete set of records, fully totalled and cross-referenced. This should certainly save you money, because you do not then have to pay for the accountant's time in adding up columns of figures, or searching through piles of invoices trying to tie them up to the payments and receipts shown on the bank statement. If you decide to follow this approach, the really essential material is set out up to Chapter 19, although reading the remaining chapters will help you to understand what your accountant then does for you.

Alternatively you can deal with your own tax affairs. The records produced under the system here are designed so that they will produce the figures you will need to enter on your tax return, which has to be sent each year to HM Revenue & Customs. Chapters 20 to 22 explain, step by step, how to get from your end of year totals to the figures on your self-assessment tax return. It is not unrealistic for a small business owner to consider doing this without an accountant, as long as he or she proceeds carefully and methodically and recognizes when help is needed.

For many small businesses, it is not necessary to produce a 'full' set of accounts, which means drawing up a statement of your business assets and liabilities (a Statement of Financial Position, sometimes called a balance sheet) in addition to the statement that shows the profits or losses from the business (the Income Statement, sometimes called the profit and loss account). However, your bank manager may wish to see a Statement of Financial Position, and so Chapters 23 and 24 explain how you can use the system to produce one. If you want to get an overdraft facility from your bank you may also be asked to draw up a cash-flow forecast, showing how much cash you expect to receive and pay out of your business, and when. Chapter 25 explains how to do that.

Finally, how should you set a price for the goods or services that you offer? Research shows that owner-managed businesses do not normally fail because they overprice themselves, and that precisely the opposite may be true. There is, in fact, a much greater business risk in trying to compete only on price, and setting prices too low. This leads to the very common experience in small businesses of the owner being rushed off his or her feet with work, and yet still being in trouble with the bank because the finances are up against the overdraft limit. This is sometimes referred to as the 'Busy Fool' syndrome. One of the keys to successful pricing is to understand how your business costs work, and the basic techniques that accountants are taught about costing are outlined for you in Chapter 26.

The suggested way to use this book is first to read it through to Chapter 16, covering all the basic entries that every business needs to make in its book-keeping records. Then read Chapters 17 and 18 if these apply to your business, and Chapter 27 if you are thinking of using a computer. If you need information about cash-flow and pricing immediately (if you are preparing a business plan, for example) then read Chapters 25 and 26. The most useful time to read Chapters 19 to 24 may be a few months after you have started keeping records under this system, so that you already have a clear understanding of what is involved. You can then decide for yourself whether you need professional help with your end of year accounts and your personal tax return.

Focus points

You can use this book if you are:

* a sole trader or small partnership
* with only one bank account
* without too many sales and purchases on credit.

Everyone should read up to and including Chapter 16. Read the other chapters if and when you need them. For example:

* Chapter 17: details about VAT
* Chapter 18: what to do if you need to pay wages
* Chapter 19: year-end summarizing
* Chapters 20–22: for help with your tax return
* Chapters 23–24: creating a Statement of Financial Position
* Chapter 25: creating a cash flow forecast
* Chapter 26: setting prices
* Chapter 27: using a computer to help with your accounting

Your bank account

In this chapter you will learn:

▶ *Why you need a business bank account*
▶ *How to check your recording system*
▶ *How to read your bank statements*

Why you need a business bank account

For a small part-time business where customers pay in cash, a separate bank account for the business might not be needed. However, many successful businesses use a second personal bank account to undertake their business transactions. In that case a modified version of the simple cashbook system, described in Chapter 3, can be used to record income and expenses. Once the number of business transactions rises above about a dozen or so each month (both purchases and sales combined) a more formal system for the recording and analysis of transactions is needed. By using a bank account solely for the business, separate from the owner's personal bank account, it is much easier to check the accounting records against the business bank statement, since all transactions must appear both in the records and on the bank statement. This is one of the two key checks that ensure mistakes have not been made in writing up the accounting records. The other check is that this book-keeping method has an automatic cross-checking process built into it, as explained in Chapter 4.

Another good reason for using a separate business bank account is that it provides a degree of independent evidence for HM Revenue & Customs. Tax inspectors are wary of businesses conducted wholly or mainly in cash. The visibility of a cheque or debit card payment paid out through a bank account for an amount that matches a supplier's invoice for goods purchased will be more convincing than the evidence of the invoice alone, and will help the tax inspector to gain confidence that business transactions have been recorded fully.

Remember this

Sole traders can legitimately use bank accounts in your own name – i.e. personal accounts – unless the bank's rules expressly disallow this, but do use personal savings accounts for any spare business cash as you will almost always see better interest rates that way.

It is therefore recommended that you open a separate bank account just for your business transactions. If you do decide to open a designated business account, the bank may give you free banking for the first year. After that period, charges can be as high as £1 for each cheque you write (although if you shop around you should be able to get this considerably lower), and a similar amount for each credit paid into the account. Automated electronic transactions such as direct debits and standing orders can be cheaper, or even free for some internet-based accounts; paying in cash over the counter may be even more expensive.

However, since many private bank accounts in the UK do not suffer bank charges at all, many people choose to use a second personal account to handle business transactions. Provided that the number of transactions is not high for a private account, banks may turn a blind eye even though it is likely to be in their rules that you shouldn't do this (the desperate need for income post-banking crisis is producing a tightening of these rules, however, so watch out). A useful way to minimize the number of cheques written is to use a credit card during the month to settle as many expenses as possible, and then to make a single payment to the credit card company when the statement arrives. Keeping the number of cheques paid in to an account to a minimum is more difficult, and if you pay in a lot of cash on a regular basis you will almost certainly be asked to convert to a business account because of the higher costs to the bank of handling cash.

Apart from the number of transactions, there are two other reasons why you might need a designated business account. The first is if you trade under a name other than your own. Banks normally accept cheques made payable only to the named account holder for a personal account. The second reason is if your business needs an overdraft facility. Banks will invariably ask why borrowing facilities are required, and are unlikely to grant business overdraft facilities for a personal account.

Case studies

So, how do the businesses in the case studies organize their banking needs?

Grace Morris would not be able to pay a cheque made out to 'Village Stores' into her personal account. In any case she needs to be able to pay in quite a lot of cash and to accept card payments.

She has therefore chosen a former building society that offers free business banking, as long as the account remains in credit, which includes facilities for paying in cash locally and which offers a card machine for a low fee. The account is in the name of 'Grace Morris t/a Village Stores'. The abbreviation 't/a' means 'trading as', allowing her to pay in cheques that are made out to either 'G Morris' or to 'Village Stores'. This can save her a lot of hassle in getting cheques redone when people use the wrong name.

Hardip Singh trades under his own name, but needs an overdraft facility to allow him to pay suppliers for materials and labour that he can bill to the customer only once a building job is completed. He therefore needs a business account with a bank. He did not go to the bank that holds his personal account, however, but instead asked other local builders. He found that several of them used a bank that had a branch in the local high street and where the staff understood the financial issues that face all builders. He also knew that it can make sense to keep business and private banking arrangements completely separate. It is a good idea to ask people in the same business sector and the same area for their recommendations.

Like Mrs Morris, Ben Martin cannot use a personal account because of the amount of cash that he banks each day. However, if he worked mainly for Cab-U-Like clients, so that most of his bankings came in the form of a single monthly bank transfer from Cab-U-Like, he might have been able to utilize a private account. However, given the cash factor, Mr Martin also uses a business bank account at a high street bank. He chooses one he can access easily so he can regularly bank cash he receives.

If you decide to use a business bank account because your business has a trading name distinct from your own name, but you do not have many transactions passing through it and do not need an overdraft, business accounts are available that offer free in-credit banking provided you keep below a certain number of transactions each month. Some also pay interest on positive balances. It is worth investing a little research time on the internet or in contacting local banks to determine what deals are currently available as they are constantly changing.

Bank statements and how to read them

For the bank account being used for business transactions, ask the bank to send statements each month. For a business with many transactions it may be very helpful to receive statements each week.

Remember this

Some banks now charge for paper accounts. If yours does, consider using the internet access instead to print out a 'statement' each month to check against your accounts. This will be free.

Business bank accounts generally have separate cheque-books and paying-in books. These are available in various formats, each one suitable for a different type of business. Always try to use the bound paying-in book for making and recording bank deposits; if instead you use a loose paying-in slip at the bank you risk losing the counterfoil, which forms an important part of the record-keeping system.

Remember this

Always complete the counterfoil when paying in. This is an important part of your accounting system. Also, always make sure the bank stamps this clearly so you have a receipt of your transaction in case of a query in the future.

A bank statement for a business account is similar to that for a personal account, but you do need to understand what the various entries mean. Figure 2.1 shows a typical bank statement.

A There are at least two key numbers on the statement. The first is the account number itself, which uniquely identifies the account within the bank. This is usually an eight-digit number (although at least one high street bank uses only seven for many of its accounts, somewhat confusingly!). The second is the so-called 'sort code', a six-digit number in the form xx – xx – xx, which uniquely identifies the bank branch

• ANYBANK PLC •

STATEMENT OF ACCOUNT

Mr A. N. Other
1 Avenue Road
ANYTOWN
AA1 1ZZ

Account number 765 432 10   Sort Code 12 - 34 - 56 **(A)**

Date	Details	Payments	Receipts	Balance **(B)**
20IX				
1 Sept	Balance b/f			256.09
5 Sept	Cheque 300321 **(C)**	100.00		156.09
6 Sept	Cash/cheques **(D)**		326.00	482.09
10 Sept	D/D Friary BS **(E)**	495.00		–12.91 **(G)**
13 Sept	Bank credit **(F)**		643.93	631.02
20 Sept	Bank charges **(H)**	32.00		599.02
23 Sept	Cheque 300224	154.00		445.02
30 Sept	Balance c/f **(I)**			445.02

Figure 2.1 A typical bank statement.

that holds the account. The sort code may not always appear on the statement, but it will always be printed in the upper right-hand corner of each cheque. The account number will always be on the statement.

Remember this

You will also usually find IBAN and SWIFT codes on your statements. These are not generally important for UK transactions but become important if you are doing international transactions, as they help route the transactions correctly.

B Most statements will follow a five-column layout – although some banks have changed the design of their statements to try and make them more 'user friendly'. From the left, these record the date each transaction was recorded by the bank, very basic details of each transaction, amounts paid out of the account, receipts paid into the account and the bank balance after each day's transactions.

C   Cheque payments are rarely shown with any detail other than the cheque number. For that reason it is important that you fill in the cheque-book stub accurately to show what the cheque was paid for. This is dealt with in more detail in Chapter 6.

D   Receipts shown are even less informative. Some banks number the paying-in slips, others do not. If they do not, the only information you have to go on is the amount paid in and the date of the transaction. This again means that it is essential to record the right information on the paying-in counterfoil. This is dealt with in Chapter 13.

E   Standing orders and direct debits can be shown in different ways, usually by abbreviations such as 'DD' or 'SO', or by words such as 'by order of'. While you will see information about the payee, you may not immediately recognize a payment, particularly if it is infrequent, for example an annual subscription to a trade association. It is therefore a good idea to review direct debits and standing orders regularly, to ensure that you know what each is for and that all are still valid.

F   Many businesses make or receive payments through automatic clearing systems, such as when a debit card is used. Conversely some customers may make all payments directly into your bank account, and ask for the sort code and your account number. They will notify you when payment has been made by bank transfer, moving the money automatically from their account to yours.

G   The daily balance shows whether the account is overdrawn or in credit (meaning it has a positive balance). The former is generally indicated by the use of a minus sign, or the self-explanatory letters 'OD'. The letters 'CR' show a credit (positive) balance, whereas 'DR' indicates a debit or overdrawn balance.

H The bank may also have applied charges for operating the account, charged interest for overdrafts, or made a charge for dishonoured ('bounced') cheques, which will be shown in the payments column. Always review the charges on the account for reasonableness, and contact your bank and query the calculation of anything that looks incorrect.

For example, Hardip Singh has agreed with his bank that his account has an overdraft facility of up to £10,000 at an interest rate of 5%. It is worth noting that banks will request some form of formal security or guarantee to ensure that if the business fails they can recover what is owed to them. For the past quarter (three-month period) say the account had been charged with £130 in interest charges. Looking at the statements, Hardip had been overdrawn for most of the quarter, on average by about £10,000. Now £10,000 at 5% would be £500 in interest charges per year, which, when divided by four, gives a broad estimate of £125 for the quarter. This is quite close to the figure of £130 that has been charged, and therefore looks reasonable. Had the interest charge been, say, £250, then a conversation with his bank would have been advisable.

I The statement starts with the bank balance 'brought forward' and ends with the one 'carried forward' to the next period. By definition the figures shown on the statement cannot take into account any payments that have not yet been shown on the statement, nor any bankings that have not yet been processed.

Internet banking

Internet banking, available for businesses as well as for individuals, lets you view your account balances, transfer funds between accounts, and pay bills and wages online. Online bank statements are also available. This is likely to be the favoured way to do banking now for all small businesses. It will almost certainly be the cheapest and means you can do much of your banking at a time to suit you – not just when your local branch is open. Of course, you still need to visit a branch to pay in cash or cheques.

To help prevent fraud, different banks use their own unique systems for customer identification, passwords, PIN numbers and security questions. Logging in online and making payments online requires entry of the correct security codes.

Remember this

Some banks now issue small electronic devices to compute these codes dynamically (i.e. they change each time you use them). This further increases online security.

It follows that the same degree of care must be used to keep account security safe as you would use for any online financial transaction. That said, internet banking can provide small businesses with a number of advantages in terms of ready access to their bank accounts, rapid processing of bills, ability to set up payments in advance, change standing orders and direct debits, and so on. Many businesses find using internet banking improves their efficiency in handling their accounts.

Focus points

✳ A separate bank account for the business can be useful, although it doesn't have to be what the banks call a 'business account'.

✳ Some banks offer permanent free banking for smaller businesses, subject to a limit on the number and/or value of transactions.

✳ Some banks offer good terms for a limited period when you open the account. Do watch out for what happens when these terms expire however to make sure you are not worse off in the long run with this choice.

✳ Be familiar with what the entries on your bank statement mean.

✳ Always make a rough check for reasonableness of any charges and any overdraft interest appearing on the statement.

✳ Check out the internet banking options your bank offers – they could save you lots of time and transaction fees.

A simple cashbook

In this chapter you will learn:

- ▶ *How a cashbook operates*
- ▶ *How to enter your transactions in a cashbook*

The last chapter explained how to read a bank statement and understand what all the entries mean. This chapter shows how to record the entries in a simple accounting book, called a cashbook. Confusingly, a cashbook does not normally show what has happened to the cash in your business, it shows what has happened to money you have paid into or taken out of the bank. If you want to think of it as a bank book that is fine, but it is referred to here as a cashbook because that is what it will be called by an accountant or tax inspector.

In essence, a cashbook is not much more than a detailed bank statement. It brings together in a single business record all the information normally put on cheque-book stubs and paying-in slips to identify exactly what payments have been made and what receipts have been received.

Hardip Singh's simple cashbook

In Chapter 1 you met Hardip Singh, a builder. Figure 3.1 shows his bank statement for the month of June.

The following further information is as recorded by him on his cheque-book stubs, plus it shows the regular standing orders paid out from the account.

▶ Debit card was used to High St Garage for diesel for his van.

▶ Cheque 1000235 was to the Anytown Courier for an advertisement.

▶ Cheque 1000236 was to Browns for stationery.

▶ Debit card was to Smarts Builders' Merchants for supplies, of which £30 was for use in his own home.

- Cheque 1000237 was to Jones Plumbing for supplies.

- Debit card was to Post Office Limited for car tax (Road Fund Licence) on the van.

- Cheque 1000238 was to Print Presto for business cards and letterheads.

- The standing order payment to County Leasing is the monthly instalment on the lease contract for the van, and the payment to Magnificent Mutual is for his personal pension.

- The direct debit payment to NICO is to the National Insurance Contributions Office for his Class 2 National Insurance Contributions (NICs). Your total might not be the same as Hardip's is here, as this varies from year to year.

		Debit	Credit	Balance
1 June	Balance b/f			2150.25
3 June	s/o County Leasing	345.22		1805.03
8 June	Card payment	28.34		1776.69
10 June	Dep 6000132		396.75	2173.44
10 June	Ch 1000236	25.68		2147.76
12 June	s/o H. Singh	500.00		1647.76
14 June	Charges	42.30		1605.46
18 June	Ch 1000235	43.69		1561.77
18 June	Card payment	692.59		869.18
20 June	Dep 6000133		2750.00	3619.18
21 June	DD NICO	28.40		3590.78
23 June	Ch 1000237	254.00		3336.78
23 June	Card payment	150.00		3186.78
28 June	Ch 1000238	82.38		3104.40
30 June	DD Mag. Mutual	100.00		3004.40
30 June	Balance b/f			3004.40

Figure 3.1 Hardip Singh's bank statement.

▶ The payment to H. Singh is the money he takes out of the business each month for his living needs and private use; it is known as monthly 'Drawings' and is paid into his personal bank account.

Remember this

If you are operating a separate bank account for your business you should be strict with yourself and only put business transactions through this account – and *all* business transactions – so there is a clear separation between your personal transactions and your business ones. This will make your accounting much easier to do.

Mr Singh issues an invoice from a pre-numbered duplicate book for each building job done.

▶ Deposit number 6000132 was a cheque from Mr Henderson paying invoice 121.

▶ Deposit 6000133 was a cheque for £2,000 from Mr Peters paying invoice number 118, a cheque for £600 from Dr Bull paying invoice number 119 and £150 in cash from Mr Blunt paying invoice number 123.

Mr Singh writes his cashbook up at the end of each month when he receives his bank statement. He uses a two-column cashbook, so that he can enter subtotals, and he writes receipts on the left-hand page and payments on the right. Figure 3.2 shows his Payments page for June.

▶ Notes

1 Each entry shows if it was paid by debit card, the cheque number, the payee to whom the payment was made, and the type of expense (shown in brackets). Some of these will be obvious; for example Road Fund Licence and fuel are classed as 'Motor'. Some will not be so obvious, such as 'Cost of sales'. The reason for using these specific headings rather than choosing ones that may be more appropriate to Mr Singh's business is that they are the ones he will need to use when filling in his tax return. By using these categories right

PAYMENTS

3 June	s/o County Leasing	(Motor)		345.22
8 June	Card High St Garage	(Motor)		28.34
10 June	236 V G Browns	(Administration)		25.68
12 June	s/o H. Singh	(Drawings)		500.00
14 June	Charges	(Finance charges)		42.30
18 June	235 Anytown Courier	(Advertising)		43.69
18 June	Card Smarts	(Cost of Sales)	662.59	
	Card Smarts	(Drawings)	30.00	692.59
21 June	DD NICO	(Drawings)		28.40
23 June	237 Jones Plumbing	(Cost of Sales)		254.00
23 June	Card Post Office Limited	(Motor)		150.00
28 June	241 Print Presto	(Administration)		82.38
30 June	DD Magnificent Mutual	(Drawings)		100.00
30 June	Total			2292.60

Figure 3.2 Hardip Singh's payments.

from the start, filling in the tax return will be made much easier. The types of payment to be included in each category are set out in the next chapter.

2 Money taken out of the business for the owner's personal use is 'Drawings' and this will include payments to the owner's pension plan, and any tax and national insurance payments. The latter are not expenses of the business, they are the owner's private liability.

3 As long as cheques run in a numerical sequence from one cheque-book to the next, only the last three digits may be needed.

4 The total payment to Smarts included £30 of materials that were for Mr Singh's private usage, and so must be recorded as drawings. Be careful always to do this when you take materials for your own use or you'll get into trouble with your tax reporting where you must get this right. Two cashbook entries are thus made for the same cheque, with amounts in the first column that add up to

the subtotal amount of the cheque, which is entered in the second column.

5 All the payments shown are inclusive of any VAT charged.

Mr Singh's Receipts page (i.e. the left-hand page to his cashbook) for June is shown in Figure 3.3.

RECEIPTS			
1 June	Brought forward		2150.25
10 June	132 Henderson (Invoice 121)		396.75
20 June	133 Peters (Invoice 118)	2000.00	
	133 Bull (Invoice 119)	600.00	
	133 Blunt (Invoice 123)	150.00	2750.00
30 June	TOTAL		5297.00
	Less payments		2292.60
			3004.40

Figure 3.3 Hardip Singh's receipts.

▶ Notes

1 Mr Singh writes up his records only when he receives his monthly bank statement, and so the balance brought forward of £2150.25 will be the same in his cashbook and on the bank statement. It is included on the 'Receipts' side of the page because he is in credit at the bank. As a result of previous transactions there have been £2,150.25 more receipts than payments. If he had been overdrawn the balance would be brought forward on the 'Payments' side.

2 After the entries have been totalled, the total from the Payments page of £2,292.60 is deducted, to give the balance carried forward of £3,004.40.

3 In this example the bankings for each separate invoice have been listed and totalled. Although this is the clearest way of entering the information, it is not always possible if there are many small receipts. You will learn the different ways

that receipts can be recorded in Chapter 14, and there is an example showing daily takings later in this chapter.

4   The fact that some of the receipts were in cash and some were cheques does not matter, since they were all paid in to the bank. When cash received is not all paid in to the bank, a way has to be found of entering it in the cashbook, as will be explained in the next example.

Ben Martin's cashbook

Ben Martin writes up his cashbook every week, even though he receives bank statements only monthly. He keeps a list of his standing orders, and he uses this plus his cheque-book stubs and paying-in book stubs to write up his cashbook. As a taxi driver, most of his sales are in cash, which he banks each weekday after taking out £30 per day as drawings. During the first week of May he wrote three cheques: one to pay off the charge card with which he purchases fuel, one to pay for the hire of his vehicle, and one to pay for an advertisement in *Yellow Pages*. He also knows that a monthly payment to the Cab Drivers Benevolent Fund has been paid by standing order. Figure 3.4 shows his Payments page for the week:

PAYMENTS			
1 May	Cab Drivers Benevolent	(Drawings)	10.00
3 May	334 Freeway Chargecard	(Cost of sales)	143.80
3 May	335 Taxicab Leasing	(Motor)	350.00
6 May	336 Yellow Pages	(Advertising)	140.00
7 May	Cash contra	(Drawings)	150.00
	TOTAL		793.80

Figure 3.4 Ben Martin's payments.

▶ **Notes on Payments**

1   The dates are the dates that he wrote the cheques and the date that the standing orders are due to go out. Be aware that they will not necessarily be banked in this order by the recipients, and so the balance on Mr Martin's cashbook

will not always tie up with the balance shown by the bank statement. The process of checking which cheques and deposits have not yet cleared through the bank account is known as the bank reconciliation and is explained in Chapter 16.

2   There may be other payments or receipts which have gone through the bank account, bank charges for example, which Mr Martin will become aware of only when he receives the bank statement. These will be entered in the cashbook as part of the bank reconciliation.

3   Mr Martin's fuel costs are categorized as 'Cost of sales' rather than 'Motor' costs. This is what HM Revenue & Customs require of taxi drivers and others in the transport industry, where costs of fuel are what is known as a 'direct' cost, that is, directly related to the amount of income that is earned. One reason for this is that the tax inspector would expect fuel costs to be a broadly similar proportion of takings for all taxi drivers, and knowing that might then be able to identify individual sets of taxi driver accounts where the declared income figures looked somewhat low.

4   The item 'Cash contra' relates to the daily £30 personal drawings taken out of business takings. It may not immediately be obvious why this item needs to be entered in the cashbook, but the Receipts page shown as Figure 3.5 reveals why.

▶ Notes on Receipts

1   It would be impractical to enter each separate fare that Mr Martin received and so the whole day's takings are entered as a single figure.

2   Total takings on 7 May, for example, were £110.60. However, only £80.60 of this total was banked. If the only figure entered into the cashbook was the £80.60, then takings, and thus Mr Martin's profit, would be understated by £30. Another way to get around this issue might be to pay all daily takings into the bank and then for Mr Martin

RECEIPTS			
1 May	Balance b/f		2496.92
3 May	Takings banked	116.67	
	plus cash contra	30.00	146.67
4 May	Takings banked	68.56	
	plus cash contra	30.00	98.56
5 May	Takings banked	94.63	
	plus cash contra	30.00	124.63
6 May	Takings banked	72.49	
	plus cash contra	30.00	102.49
7 May	Takings banked	80.60	
	plus cash contra	30.00	110.60
	TOTAL		3079.87
	Less payments		793.80
	Balance c/f		2286.07

Figure 3.5 Ben Martin's receipts.

to take out the £30 drawings needed for his daily living needs from the bank. However, that might then result in unnecessary additional bank charges.

The approach adopted by Mr Martin is to write up his cashbook as if all takings had been banked. So-called contra entries are used to do this, 'contra' meaning that there are corresponding entries on both the receipts and payments sides of the cashbook, and these effectively balance each other out. On the 'Receipts' page the cash drawings are added back to the takings to arrive at the full amount Mr Martin received from carrying passengers and, as we have already seen, on the Payments page the £30 a day is entered as a payment out. These can be entered daily as here or shown as a weekly total. To illustrate both approaches, a daily entry has been shown on the Receipts page and the weekly total on the Payments page, although in practice it is better to be consistent on both sides of the cashbook so that the corresponding contra entries can be easily identified.

When to update the cashbook

There are two possible ways of updating the cashbook. It can either be prepared from the bank statement, as in Hardip Singh's case, or it can be written up as you go along, and then reconciled to the bank statement when it comes in, as Ben Martin does. Different approaches will suit different businesses.

One advantage of updating the cashbook once the bank statement is received is that it is easier to compare the two. The final balance shown on the cashbook should always agree with the final balance on the statement. This makes it easier to identify mistakes. It may also take less time to sit down for a couple of hours each month with all the necessary records to hand and update the cashbook in one go, rather than spending time doing it each day or even once per week.

Conversely, the advantage of keeping the cashbook up to date as you go along is that you always know what your true balance at the bank is, if all cheques you have written or debit card payments made had been cashed and if all bankings made had been credited to the account. This lets you keep a helpful daily or weekly running total in pencil in the margin.

Remember this

Because it may take an hour or two, it may be tempting to put off the job of updating the cashbook, and therefore some people find that a regular but quicker daily (or weekly) update routine is easier to stick to. As a general rule, the more important it is to know how much money you have at, or owe to, the bank, the better it will be to update the cashbook as you go along.

Cashbook analysis

The cashbook provides the most fundamental financial record for each business. However, it won't immediately show the owner how the receipts and payments under various different headings combine overall. By looking back at Mr Singh's cashbook, it is quite easy to see how a statement showing his receipts and payments could be prepared from it. Total receipts in the month were £3,146.75, being the £5,297.00 total shown on the Receipts page of the cashbook less the £2,150.25 that he had started with at the beginning of the month (see Figure 3.3). For payments, the various entries on the Payments page can be totalled using their various expense categories, as shown in Figure 3.6.

Motor	(345.22 + 28.34 + 150)	£523.56
Administration	(25.68 + 82.38)	£108.06
Drawings	(500 + 30 + 28.40 + 100)	£658.40
Finance charges		£42.30
Advertising		£43.69
Cost of sales	(662.59 + 254)	£916.59

Figure 3.6 Hardip Singh – expenses.

Even with the limited number of transactions going through Mr Singh's accounts, it is still easy to miss one when calculating the totals. Once the number of transactions per month exceeds perhaps 30, then the likelihood of an error being made could be quite high.

In order to simplify the process of calculating totals for each category and for each month, the simple two-column cashbook can be expanded so that each amount is recorded first of all in a total column, and then secondly in a separate column set up for each individual expense or receipt category. This format is commonly known as an 'analysed cashbook', and is at the heart of the accounting system set out in this book. The detailed format of the analysed cashbook will be examined in the next chapter.

Focus points

✳ A simple (two-column) cashbook may be all you need as the core of your book-keeping system if you have fewer than 12 or so transactions a month.

✳ A cashbook shows what has gone in to and out of your bank account.

✳ Update your cashbook as you go along (and reconcile to bank statements when received) or prepare from the bank statement when you receive it. Either way is fine *but* it is vital you keep it up to date so you have a good idea how much money you have at any point.

Analysis columns

In this chapter you will learn:

▶ *How to create analysis columns*
▶ *The different expense categories*

Layout

Figure 4.1 shows how the payments side of Mr Singh's original two-column cashbook, as seen in the last chapter, would look when set out in full analysed cashbook format. If this looks somewhat daunting simply compare it with Figure 3.2 and you will find that the differences are really quite straightforward.

The first two columns of the analysed cashbook are almost exactly the same as the first two columns of the simple cashbook, showing the date and the details of the payments from the bank statement. The only difference is that the category of expenditure (motor, drawings, etc.) is no longer recorded in brackets when writing up the details. The third column of the analysed cashbook is exactly the same as the last column of the two-column cashbook: it shows amounts paid out of the bank account, just as before.

However, you will now notice additional columns on the right of the 'Total' column, each one headed up with one of the categories of expenditure, the categories previously recorded as part of the details of the payment in the original simple cashbook. There were six categories used, so six additional columns are needed to do the analysis.

Looking at the first entry, £345.22 paid to County Leasing for van rental, which was categorized in the two-column cashbook as 'Motor'. In the analysed cashbook, as well as the sum of £345.22 being entered in the 'Total' column, it is also entered under the 'Motor' column.

The next payment is the debit card payment to High St Garage. This is also a motoring expense, so £28.34 is entered in the 'Total' column and under the 'Motor' column.

The next payment is to V G Browns for stationery, categorized in the two-column cashbook as 'Administration'. In the analysed cashbook, the amount paid out of £25.68 is entered in both the 'Total' column and in the 'Administration' column.

All the other entries are made in the same way, but note particularly the entry for 18 June, debit card payment to Smarts. The total of £692.59 was made up of £30 for goods

Date	Details	Total	Motor	Admin.	Drawings	Finance	Advertising	Cost of sales
3 Jun	s/o County Leasing	345.22	345.22					
8 Jun	Card High St Garage	28.34	28.34					
10 Jun	236 V G Browns	25.68		25.68				
12 Jun	s/o H Singh	500.00			500.00			
14 Jun	Charges	42.30				42.30		
18 Jun	235 Anytown Courier	43.69					43.69	
18 Jun	Card Smarts	692.59			30.00			662.59
21 Jun	DD NICO	28.40			28.40			
23 Jun	237 Jones Plumb.	254.00						254.00
23 Jun	Card Post Office Ltd.	150.00	150.00					
28 Jun	238 Print Presto	82.38		82.38				
30 Jun	DD Magnificent Mutual	100.00			100.00			
30 Jun	TOTALS	2,292.60	523.56	108.06	658.40	42.30	43.69	916.59

Figure 4.1 Hardip Singh – analysed payments for June.

used privately, categorized as 'Drawings', with the balance of £662.59 reflecting the cost of materials used on a building job, categorized as 'Cost of sales'. In the simple cashbook these were entered as separate figures and then totalled up. However, in the analysed cashbook, the full £692.59 is entered in the 'Total' column, then £30.00 entered under 'Drawings' and £662.59 entered under 'Cost of sales'. Note carefully that exactly the same information is recorded, but the way that it is set out under each method is different.

Figure 4.1 illustrates an important point about analysed cashbooks. For each entry, the total of the amounts entered in the detailed analysis columns will be exactly the same as the amount entered in the total column. Provided a business is not VAT-registered (we will talk about VAT in Chapter 17), most entries will have only one amount in an analysis column, which matches the amount in the 'Total' column. If, as for the Smarts entry, the expenditure relates to more than one category, the total under all of the separate columns will always add up to the amount shown by the 'Total' column.

Looking at the totals, it now becomes clear that it is quite easy for Mr Singh to add up the expenditure under each category heading, and that is the main reason for using separate analysis columns. For example, when using the two-column cashbook there were four different entries categorized as 'Drawings' scattered over the page. Making sure that he didn't miss any in calculating the total for drawings in Figure 3.6 could have been difficult, especially if there had been 50 entries rather than 12. By using an analysed cashbook Mr Singh must simply add up the figures in each column in order to arrive at total expenditure in the month for each category. If you compare the payments summary in Figure 3.2 with the totals for each column in Figure 4.1, you will see that they match.

Another important point to note is that when added together the totals of the analysis columns will be the same as the total of the 'Total' column. In other words, looking at Figure 4.1, £(523.56 + 108.06 + 658.40 + 42.30 + 43.69 + 916.59) gives a total of £2,292.60. If this cross-checking process does not work then an error must have occurred somewhere.

Expense categories

As noted in Chapter 3, the column headings for analysis by this system are based around the categories required by HM Revenue & Customs in the UK self-assessment tax return. These are listed below, together with details of what should be included under each heading. Some will be self-evident, others may be slightly surprising, and you may want to return to this chapter on occasion in order to decide which standard category covers a particular expense item.

The UK self-assessment tax return assumes that you will enter all business expenditure in the accounts, and then separately identify those expenses (entertaining, for example) that are not allowable for tax purposes. Alternatively you could choose to classify any non-tax-allowable expenses as personal drawings, which are not allowable expenses for tax purposes anyway. The general rule is that you cannot claim an expense unless it is incurred 'wholly and exclusively' for business purposes. There are many grey areas, however, and it may be wise to take advice from a suitably qualified accountant if you are unsure. The expense must also be what is known as a 'revenue' item, not 'capital'. Chapter 8 gives some basic guidance in this area, and the different treatment for tax purposes for capital items, such as the purchase of equipment, is dealt with in Chapter 9.

The following broad descriptions of the category headings are a starting point:

▶ The 'Cost of sales' category should be used for costs of supplies and raw materials that are used directly in making a product or delivering a service. Cab drivers and transport businesses would normally include their fuel costs here in view of the nature of their businesses, but for most others the costs of fuel would be what is known as an 'overhead' and allocated into the category of motor expenses.

▶ The 'Subcontractors' heading should be used only by businesses in the construction industry for payments to subcontractors. Payments to subcontract staff in other businesses, such as payments to a locum vet or GP, should be allocated to employee costs.

▶ 'Other direct costs': there are relatively few expenses that fall into this category. Include hire costs of machinery here (other than motor vehicles) and rechargeable expenses. These are any expenses that you incur but which you subsequently recover from customers. If you are not sure whether an expense belongs here or in another category, it is probably the latter.

▶ 'Employee costs' consist of not just employee salaries, but (as noted above) payments to subcontractors other than construction industry subcontractors, and payments to recruitment agencies for any temporary or contract staff. Do not include what you may refer to as your own 'wages'; these are in fact drawings from the business. Note that it may be worthwhile in tax terms to pay a salary to a partner/

spouse, but you must be able to show HMRC that the work performed is genuinely worth the payment made, and an accountant's advice should always be sought if you are unsure.

▶ 'Premises' costs include rent, heat, light and insurance. For the typical small business operating from the owner's home, an adjustment at the end of the year for what is known as 'use of home as office' may be all that is needed. This is covered in Chapter 22.

▶ 'Repairs' covers both the maintenance of business premises and machinery repairs. Note that any 'improvements' cannot be claimed against tax, and so professional advice may be needed when, for example, replacing old office windows with new uPVC ones, where there is both a 'repairs' element and an 'improvement' element.

▶ 'General administrative expenses' is a catch-all heading for office expenses such as telephone, stationery, postage and business subscriptions. This is where a lot of expenses for most businesses will end up.

▶ 'Motor expenses' are relatively self-explanatory, but note that car repairs will normally go here, not under the repairs category.

▶ 'Travel and subsistence' costs include any travel other than motor expenses, plus the cost of any hotel accommodation while away on business trips. There are specific rules about claiming for meals and subsistence, and these will be worth checking if you stay away on business to ensure that you claim as much as is legitimately possible. Remember always that if you don't claim for a cost that you are entitled to claim for, it is unlikely that the tax inspector will suggest that you should be claiming it! Not least, he or she will probably be unaware that you have incurred it.

▶ The 'Advertising' heading also includes cost of direct mail and promotional activity. Entertainment costs for customers and suppliers is never tax allowable, although entertainment of employees can be allowable up to a maximum amount per employee per year.

- ▶ 'Legal and professional fees' will include payments to lawyers, accountants and architects, for example. You cannot, however, claim against income tax the costs of fees or fines for breaking the law, nor fees which relate to the purchase of fixed assets such as machinery or property.

- ▶ 'Interest' costs should be self-explanatory.

- ▶ 'Other finance charges' relates to bank and other finance costs other than interest charges.

- ▶ 'Other business expenses' is another broad category, but as noted earlier many general expenses will fall under the general administrative costs heading.

- ▶ 'Drawings' will include all payments that are for private purposes rather than business costs. This includes the owner's tax and national insurance bill.

- ▶ 'Purchase of equipment' is dealt with in Chapter 9, but this is the heading to use to record so-called 'capital' payments where long-term assets (ones you typically will keep for more than 12 months) are being acquired, such as furniture, vehicles and equipment.

Focus points

✻ A two-column cashbook is really a bank statement with some extra explanation.

✻ An analysed cashbook is used to allocate different types of expense into different columns.

✻ In an analysed cashbook, each figure is written twice, once in total and once analysed across the expense columns.

✻ By categorizing expenses using HM Revenue & Customs' own categories, and only entering allowable expenses, completion of your tax return will be much easier.

✻ UK tax law can be complex. Always seek appropriate professional advice if you are unsure.

Payments – filing

In this chapter you will learn:

▶ *How to file invoices*
▶ *How to manage your creditors*
▶ *How to deal with suppliers' statements*

This chapter and Chapters 6 and 7 will take you step by step through the process for recording your payments. This chapter looks at filing, Chapter 6 looks at what to record in your cheque-book, and Chapter 7 looks again at the entries in the cashbook itself, concentrating on more difficult transactions. These chapters do not deal with payments made by credit card or by cash; those are dealt with in Chapters 10 and 11 respectively.

From now on you will find references in the chapters to the different items of business stationery that you will need; these are summarized in Appendix 3, as a shopping list. However, please finish this book first so that you understand exactly what you need and how you will use it.

Filing invoices

To file your invoices, use a large A4 lever-arch file, and a hole punch so that you can punch filing holes into any invoice that does not already have them. You also need divider cards: purchase a pack or simply use pieces of cardboard that are slightly larger than A4 size. You will also need a stapler and a pad of A4 paper.

The system is simple and straightforward, with three basic rules:

1 The invoices are filed in the order that you pay them, not when they are received.

2 Each invoice has written on it the date of payment and the number of the cheque sent in payment.

3 Invoices are kept on top of a dividing card while they remain unpaid, and filed underneath it when they have been paid.

EXAMPLE

It is 31 March. Grace Morris has just been to the local Cash and Carry store and purchased stock costing £856. She paid by cheque, number 456. On the way back she put petrol into her estate car, paying £20 using her debit card. When she arrived at the shop she opened the post, which contained an invoice dated 28 March from one of her suppliers, Amy's Chocolates, for £254, payable within 28 days. She filed this on top of the divider card in the lever-arch file. As she did so, she looked through the other unpaid invoices on top of the divider card, and found that she had an invoice from Browns Wholesale company, which supplies her shop's newspapers and magazines, and which is overdue for payment. She paid this, £156, with cheque number 457.

The example that follows shows the paperwork relating to these transactions (see Figure 5.1), and how Mrs Morris dealt with it.

The invoices will be filed in the order in which they were paid from the cheque book. The first cheque written by Mrs Morris was number 456, £856.00 to the Cash and Carry store. She duly wrote '456' on the invoice itself as a record, and circled it so that it could easily be seen, and added the words 'Paid 31/3'. She then filed the invoice immediately below the divider card.

The next payment she made was number 457, for £20 of petrol. She kept the till receipt as evidence of the petrol purchase, and later stapled it to a larger sheet of A4 paper, writing 'Petrol, £20' on the A4 sheet. She added 'debit card' to indicate that she settled this bill by her debit card, and 'Paid 31/3' on the A4 sheet, and filed it on top of the Cash and Carry invoice, below the divider card.

The last cheque that she wrote was number 457, for £156. She then wrote '457' and 'Paid 31/3' on the supplier invoice, tore off the remittance slip to send to Browns Wholesale with the cheque, and then filed the invoice beneath the card divider and on top of the petrol invoice. Even though this invoice dates from the end of February, it goes on top of the other invoices because the filing system follows the order in which suppliers were paid, not the order in which invoices were received. Finally she filed the invoice from Amy's Chocolates on top of the divider card awaiting payment.

Remember this

Always keep any receipts, invoices and other paperwork associated with your transactions that you are given. These are vital to prove transactions happened as you have recorded them and your accountant will need these (as may HMRC if your accounts are audited by them at any stage).

O & Q Cash and Carry
Suppliers to the trade

3 Invicta Way, Camtown CC1 2BB

Mrs Grace Morris
Village Stores

INVOICE   31.3.1X

Standard-rated Goods	456.00
Zero-rated Goods	320.20
VAT@ 17.5% on standard-rated goods	79.80
	856.00

Paid by cheque

VAT no 123 654 00   (456)
                          Paid 31/3

```
HIGH ST GARAGE

31.3.1X

Petrol        £20.00


VAT no 987 654 32
```

debit card
  Paid 31/3

Browns Wholesale

Newspapers and magazines

The Business Park, Camtown CC1 9AA

Mrs Grace Morris
Village Stores
Camtown
CC11ZZ

INVOICE   29.2.1X

Goods supplied   **156.00**

ZERO-RATED FOR VAT

VAT no 123 654 78   (457)
Payable strictly net 28 days   *paid 31/3*

AMY'S CHOCOLATES

A taste of heaven

1 Industrial Way, Slough, SL1 1AA

Mrs Grace Morris
Village Stores
Camtown
CC11ZZ

INVOICE   28.3.1X

Goods supplied   **254.00**

Price includes VAT

VAT no 123 456 78

Payable strictly net 28 days

Figure 5.1 Grace Morris's invoices.

Managing your creditors

The people to whom money is owed for goods or services supplied on credit terms are known as creditors, or collectively as accounts payable, and managing payments to accounts payable is an important part of running a business. Payment dates have a direct impact upon the bank balance.

The invoice filing system described here separates paid invoices from the unpaid ones. In many small businesses it is not necessary to have a formal system for reviewing unpaid invoices, you should just review them quickly each time you open the file. However, if you have few invoices, so that the supplier invoice file may remain unopened for weeks at a time, you will want to set up some sort of diary reminder system (e.g. putting paying invoices into your 'to do' list on the relevant days if you keep such a list), or simply make a habit of checking the file at regular intervals.

It will improve your credit rating with suppliers if you pay them on time, but unless they offer an 'early settlement discount', that is offer you a discount if you pay them promptly, there is not much point in paying them in advance of their normal terms. If you are offered 28 days to pay, take that length of time – do not pay as soon as you get the invoice. It is better for you to keep your bank balance as healthy as possible by having the money in your account. If you think about it carefully, you will realize that until you pay them, your creditors are in fact supplying interest-free funds to your business!

Remember this

Provided you do pay up on time when sums are due your creditors will be happy with this process – it is a normal part of doing business.

Supplier statements

Some suppliers will send you monthly statements, often by email these days, showing a breakdown of what you owe them. These can be a useful check for you too, but be careful not to file these as if they were invoices, or you may end up paying the same bill twice. Use statements to check that the invoices shown as unpaid on the statement are still filed as unpaid (on top of the divider card) in the supplier lever-arch file.

You might not want to pay a supplier using the remittance slip on the statement, particularly if the statement covers two or more invoices, because it can then be difficult to match up the single payment to the different amounts on the invoices. If you do have to do this (for example, because you have a lot of invoices from the same supplier that you want to pay with one bank payment) then staple the relevant invoices to the back of the statement and write the cheque number or 'paid by bank transfer' on the front of the statement, then file the whole bundle together underneath the divider card so it is clear which invoices are covered by that cheque payment.

The comments about statements also apply to 'reminders', such as a 'red' telephone bill. Even if you send back the remittance slip with the payment, make full notes about payment on the original bill and file that, stapling the red reminder to the back of the original bill.

No invoices

Not every business payment will have an invoice, but each should have some sort of supporting documentation or notes on the lever-arch file. If it is a personal payment, which is clearly marked on the cheque-book stub as drawings, then this is not so important, but it is a legal requirement that you keep business records which are sufficient to justify your business expenses.

EXAMPLE

Hardip Singh paid a neighbour £25 by cheque for the use of her garage to store some machinery for a few weeks. The neighbour did not provide any form of receipt. Mr Singh duly made a note on an A4 sheet of paper 'Paid to Mrs Owen for use of garage to store machinery, £25' and wrote on it the cheque number and the date of payment in the usual way. This was filed in the supplier lever-arch file in the same place as an invoice would have been filed. It would have been better to have obtained a receipt for the payment from Mrs Owen, but at least a supporting record was created with a clear explanation of why this was a bona fide business payment.

Remember this

This form of 'proof' is likely to be accepted by the tax authorities if asked to verify that the payment really occurred as recorded, but clearly the more paper evidence you can obtain the more convincing the case would be if ever challenged.

Focus points

✻ A simple filing system using a lever-arch file and with all documents duly annotated can work well. The result will be a steadily growing file of invoices and notes of expenses underneath the dividing card, all in cheque number order, the order in which they were paid.

✻ There may not be an invoice for every cheque, but if there is not that should be because the payment is a personal one, which will be recorded under the (non tax-deductible) drawings heading in the analysed cashbook. If the payment is a business expense but with no supporting invoice, then there is at least a sheet of paper in the right place in the lever-arch file giving full details of what the payment was for.

✻ This system makes it easy to locate the supporting paperwork for all cheque payments, and provides evidence of exactly why each payment was made if asked for (e.g. in a tax audit).

Payments –
cheque-book

In this chapter you will learn:

▶ *The importance of payment details*
▶ *What to record in your cheque-book*

While cheques are used less and less as a form of personal payment these days, they are important still for business transactions as they help to provide an audit trail if you need to prove when and how payments were made. In the last chapter there were several references to writing cheques. Completing cheques, and the cheque-book stubs correctly, is the subject of this chapter. This area may seem obvious but is actually surprisingly important to get right.

The aim of the system for recording payments is to ensure that all essential details are recorded in at least two places. In that way, if records are mislaid, such as a set of cheque-book stubs, or a file of invoices, or even your cashbook for a year, it becomes possible to reconstruct what has been lost from the other information held.

The importance of payment details

First and foremost a cheque-book stub must record the purpose of a payment. The main aim of the book-keeping system is to identify items of business income and expenses and record them under the appropriate category headings for submission to HM Revenue & Customs in due course. For example, if an electricity bill is paid by cheque, the most important thing to write on the cheque stub is 'Electricity' (or something similar) as an accurate and adequate description of what the payment was for in case you need to refer to it at a later date.

The next most important piece of information is to state to whom the cheque was paid. In the case of an electricity bill that mostly likely would be the name of your energy supplier. If a cheque stub doesn't state clearly to whom a payment has been made then it might later be misinterpreted as being for something else. Stating the purpose clearly and accurately on the stub really matters, therefore.

The cheque stub should also note the date that the invoice being paid was raised. This lets the business owner check in either the cheque-book or the supplier invoice file whether a particular purchase invoice has been paid.

Also record the date that a cheque is being paid, since the only other place that this is recorded will be in the supplier invoice file. If a cheque is being 'post-dated' (writing a date on it that is later than the current date, which is perfectly acceptable if your debt isn't due to be settled yet) record clearly both dates on the cheque stub.

Finally, note on the stub the amount that the cheque was made out for. However, if you forget you will be able to find the amount on the invoice and confirm that you made the cheque out for that amount when your bank statement arrives. In practice, most people remember to write in the amount on the stub, but it is in fact the purpose, both relevant dates, and the payee name which they may omit. It is far more difficult, and time-consuming, to get these details right later although it takes just a matter of seconds to complete them on the stub at the time that the cheque is written.

EXAMPLE
Refer again to the first example in Chapter 5, dealing with Grace Morris. Figure 6.1 shows the cheque-book stubs as she

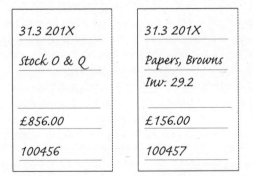

Figure 6.1 Grace Morris's cheque stubs.

filled them in. Remember that she wrote the first cheque for goods she had just purchased. These were not on credit and so she does not need to add the dates of the invoice as this is the same as the date of payment.

EXAMPLE
Refer back to Figure 3.4, showing Ben Martin's payments for the first week of May. He wrote three cheques: one paying off

a charge card for fuel costs, one for leasing the vehicle, and one for an advertisement in *Yellow Pages*. Figure 6.2 shows how he would fill in his cheque stubs.

3.5 201X	3.5 201X	6.5 201X
Petrol	Taxi lease	Advert
'Freeway'	Taxicab Leasing	Yellow Pages
Inv. 14/4	Inv. 18/4	Inv. 30/3
£143.80	£350.00	£140.00

Figure 6.2 Ben Martin's cheque stubs.

Missing details

It is quite possible that having read through the recommendations for record-keeping above, these seem to be a detailed explanation of the rather obvious. In practice, when accountants are preparing business accounts from the books and accounts of small businesses they often find that cheque-book stub details are missing or incomplete. It is also worth remembering that a scribbled note which makes perfect sense to you when you write it may not mean anything when you are asked to explain it by your tax inspector or VAT officer a year or two later. The habit of filling in your cheque stubs correctly will serve you well! You may want to note down the following five points inside the cover of your cheque-book, so that you remember to complete all the relevant details.

1 Purpose

2 Payee

3 Invoice date

4 Date written

5 Amount

If, for any reason, you do not use a cheque (if you make a mistake in writing it out, for example) then simply put a line through the cheque stub and write 'Cancelled' on it.

Old cheque-books

When you finish a cheque-book, you should store the cheque-book stubs safely. You also need to be able to find the right book quickly when you need it. At the very least, keep all the old books of stubs together, in order, fastened by an elastic band. A better approach, however, is to set up a system that will eventually hold all your accounting records for the year.

Purchase a box file, and write the tax year on the outside. In the UK the tax year ends each 5 April for historical reasons, and therefore it may be convenient to keep 31 March as your business year end, the nearest month end to the tax year. For various technical reasons, this may also help in due course with certain complexities involved in calculating your tax bill. It is assumed here that your year end is 31 March, although the final choice of year-end date must also take into account what best suits you. If in doubt please consult a qualified accountant.

The box file will now say, for example, 'Year ended 31 March 201X'. Write on the outside cover of each cheque-book the range of cheque numbers that it contains: for example '231–280'. Keep them in the box file, together with any other cheque-books that were finished during the year, bundled together with an elastic band. The box file will seem rather empty at first, but also use it to store documents like guarantees for items bought during the year and additional notes and correspondence that explain various transactions. Also keep used paying-in books here.

At the end of the year the box file will come into its own. It will become the single storage and reference point for the year for your paid purchase invoices and your sales invoices, and contain the bank statements for that year and a copy of your tax return itself. All are records that you need to keep for seven years in case of a tax or VAT inspection.

Focus points

✻ Complete your cheque-book stubs fully – you'll be glad you did later I promise!

✻ Don't throw away your old cheque-book stubs – keep them all safely somewhere where you can access them easily if needed.

Payments – cashbook

In this chapter you will learn:

▶ *More about analysis columns*

▶ *How to complete the 'payments' side of the cashbook*

This chapter builds on the information in Chapter 4 about using analysis columns to record payments. The example given in Chapter 4 showed the basic principle of the analysis into different columns; this chapter shows the method being used for a more complex example.

Buying a cashbook

Suitable analysis cashbooks are sold in stationery shops. They are approximately A3 size, the size of two standard sheets of A4 paper side by side. When opened up, the double page will resemble Figure 7.1. There is space left available at the top for the overall heading and space at the top of each column for the analysis headings. The left-most three columns are different from the others. The first will be used to record the date, the second is wider to allow for written details, such as the name of the person to whom a cheque was payable, and the third column is a narrow one, and sometimes referred to as the folio column. It would typically be used to record cheque numbers.

After that there are columns used for recording the analysed amounts. To give plenty of space, many people select a 32-column analysed cashbook, which means 32-columns in addition to the first three.

Heading up the cashbook

Inside the front cover of the book insert your name and contact details. Even if you intend to deal with your own affairs, it may be necessary at some point for the book to be sent to your accountant or for examination by HM Revenue & Customs, and clear labelling is an insurance policy against it being lost in a large office, as has been known to happen.

It is easiest to start the book at the beginning of a business year, if possible. Figure 7.2 shows how the top of the page might look after the headings have been completed. Note that only a sample of the analysis columns has been shown.

At the top of the page, write in the name of the bank, the sort code and the account number. Apart from being an easy place

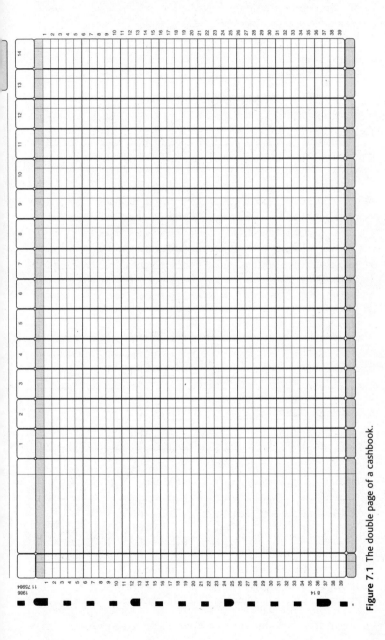

Figure 7.1 The double page of a cashbook.

Bank account no 123 456 78   Sort code 12 34 56   April 201X

Date	Payments out	Cheque number	Total	Cost of sales	Subcontract.	Other direct costs	Employee costs	Repairs	General admin.

Figure 7.2 The first page of the cashbook.

to find these details when you want them, this will prevent problems in matching up the cashbook to the bank statements if the business changes banks. Also write in the month and year, and start a new page at the beginning of each month.

Head up the left-most column as 'Date'. The next (wide) column should be labelled 'Payments out', and the small column headed 'Cheque number'.

The next column, the first monetary column, should be headed 'Total'. Leave the following column blank: you will use it later when checking off the payments to the bank statement, and to note any brought-forward bank overdraft figure. Head up the columns following with the categories listed in Chapter 4, missing out any that you will not need for your business. List them in the order that they are given in Chapter 4, which will also be the correct order for the same categories on your tax return. This may take up to the sixteenth column, depending on which headings are being used.

Leave the other columns blank, they will be used later for receipts headings, as will be explained in Chapter 14. If you are VAT-registered, you will also need a column for VAT, as will be explained in Chapter 17.

Writing up the cashbook

To start using the cashbook, enter first the latest balance shown on the bank statement, adjusting if necessary for any cheques written and deposits made before the cashbook start date but which, for timing reasons, are not reflected in the bank statement at that date. You need to make this adjustment only if you will be writing up the books from your records as you go along; if you are going to write them up when they appear on the bank statement then simply start with the opening balance on the statement.

The reason for entering the opening balance is to allow easy checking of your bank balance. Adding all the figures in a 'Payments in' (Receipts) Total column and in the 'Payments out' Total column, and then subtracting the second total from the first will give the latest bank balance, positive if the balance is in credit and negative if it is overdrawn.

If the bank balance brought forward at the start date is positive (i.e. you are in credit at the bank) this should be written in the first line of the Total column for payments in, covered in detail in Chapter 14. If the balance is overdrawn it will go in the first line of the Total column for payments out. Simply enter the date, write 'Balance b/f' (brought forward) in the details, nothing under 'Cheque number', and the balance under 'Total'.

Figure 7.3 shows the payments side of Mr Singh's cashbook again, although the balance brought forward has now been changed. More columns have been included, in the order set out in Chapter 4. The last columns, not needed for the entries given, have not been shown in order to make the illustration clearer.

Note that a balance brought forward of £2,040.53 appears on the payments side. Mr Singh's business was overdrawn by this amount according to his bank statement on 1 June. He writes up his cashbook only when he receives the bank statement and therefore does not need to adjust the opening balance for any uncleared items. The Total column now includes the 'opening' overdraft figure, and so not only shows the amount that has been spent during the month, it reveals the amount by which the business would be overdrawn if all the payments out had been made but nothing paid into the account.

Figure 7.4 shows Ben Martin's cashbook, payments side only, written up for the first week of May, the information first seen in Figure 3.4.

Ben's business was in credit at the bank, so there is no entry for a balance brought forward on the payments side of the cashbook. The other entries are as before, including the cash contra being taken to drawings. Remember that we are looking only at the payments side at present, and so it is not immediately obvious where the cash contra entry has arisen. As explained in Chapter 3, it is needed because Ben retained some cash received to spend privately, and this amount must be recorded as drawings.

Bank account no 123 456 23   Sort code 22-22-22   June 201X

Date	Payments out	Cheque no/debit card	Total	Cost of sales	Employees	Admin.	Motor	Travel	Advertising	Legal/ Prof.	Finance	Drawings
1 Jun	Bal b/f		2,040.53	2,040.53								
3 Jun	s/o County Leasing		345.22				345.22					
8 Jun	High St Garage	Debit	28.34				28.34					
10 Jun	V G Browns		25.68			25.68						
12 Jun	s/o HSingh		500.00									500.00
14 Jun	Charges		42.30								42.30	
18 Jun	Anytown Courier	235	43.69						43.69			
18 Jun	Smarts	Debit	692.59	662.59								30.00
21 Jun	DD NICO		28.40									28.40
23 Jun	Jones Plumb.	237	254.00	254.00								
23 Jun	Post Office Limited	Debit	150.00				150.00					
28 Jun	Print Presto	238	82.38			82.38						
30 Jun	d/d Magnificent Mutual		100.00									100.00
30 Jun	TOTALS		4333.13	2,040.53	916.59	108.06	523.56		43.69		42.30	658.40

Figure 7.3 Hardip Singh's payments page – June.

Bank account no 123 456 78   Sort code 33-33-33   April 201X

Date	Payments out	Cheque number	Total	Cost of sales	Admin.	Motor	Travel	Advertising	Drawings
1 May	Cab Drivers Ben.	SO	10.00						10.00
3 May	Freeway C/Card	334	143.80	143.80					
3 May	Taxicab Leasing	335	350.00			350.00			
6 May	Yellow Pages	336	140.00					140.00	
7 May	Cash contra		150.00						150.00

(Other unused columns are not shown.)

Figure 7.4 Ben Martin's payments out page – May.

Non-allowable expenses

In this chapter you will learn:

▶ *Which expenses are not allowable for tax calculations*

▶ *What expenses to include in your analysis headings*

In entering the cashbook analysis headings in Chapter 4, one method was simply to omit expense categories that were not tax allowable. This chapter reviews the types of expenditure that may not be allowable, but also highlights less obvious expenses that can be used to reduce your tax bill.

Given the scope of this book it can only cover here some of the key principles about income tax for people running self-employed businesses. To obtain more detailed information, a range of guides is published by HM Revenue & Customs, available free from your local tax office and online. Tax legislation can be very complex, however, and you should always seek help from a qualified accountant if you are in doubt.

The 'wholly and exclusively' rule

The most important general rule is that an expense will be allowable against tax only if it is incurred 'wholly and exclusively' for business purposes. When this rule is applied strictly it can be harsh. A professional guitarist was refused a deduction for the costs of an operation to correct a problem in his little finger, despite evidence that he had needed the treatment solely to improve his playing. The court held that since he also played for pleasure, the purpose of the operation was partly private. In another leading case a female barrister wore black skirts and jackets under her robes when in court. She did not wear them anywhere else because she did not like wearing black, but she was refused a tax deduction. The court held that a central motive for wearing the clothes was modesty; she would not walk down the street dressed only in her underwear and thus the clothes had a purpose that was not wholly and exclusively business-related.

Sometimes in practice, however, tax inspectors may be willing to split a cost as part business and part private on an appropriate percentage basis, but be careful about discussing any private element to any expense, since strictly speaking that disbars it from being tax allowable. (Of course, you have to be truthful and own up to any private elements if there are any – the tax inspector will not be happy to find this out later.)

Revenue expenditure versus capital expenditure

A second key tax concept is that an allowable expense must be a 'revenue' expense, broadly a cost that is charged to the business Income Statement, rather than a 'capital' item. Certain capital expenditure, mainly the purchase of plant, machinery and equipment, including vehicles, receives a separate tax relief via 'capital allowances'. Details of how to record the purchase of capital equipment are included in the next chapter, and the calculation of capital allowances is outlined. Be aware, however, that some capital expenditure receives no relief at all; the purchase costs for an office building or shop, for example, cannot be claimed against tax.

Remember this

This distinction gives rise to some unusual results. If a boiler and chimney are part of a factory, and are demolished and rebuilt, and still part of the same factory, that may be classified as a repair to the existing factory and thus be allowable as a revenue expense and deductible against taxable profits. However, if a factory has a separate building that houses the boiler and chimney, and which is completely demolished and a new one built, that is probably a capital expense.

Franchise businesses can also give rise to problems. Fees for initial training are usually classified as a capital item, because the cost incurred places the new owner in the position needed in order to carry on the business. However, ongoing training costs and refresher courses, incurred once the business is up and running, are viewed as being needed to allow the owner to continue running the business. They are thus revenue items and tax deductible. For the same reason, training expenditure to keep someone's knowledge up to date will normally be allowable against tax. A fee paid as a one-off payment for use of the franchise name may well be disallowed as capital, whereas payment of an ongoing annual fee is probably revenue, and allowable. If you are intending to set up a franchise business you should obtain clear written advice from the franchisor of any negotiations they have had with HM Revenue & Customs about the tax position of the various charges.

These two tax concepts, 'wholly and exclusively' and 'revenue versus capital', are commonly encountered sources of tax disallowances. The areas listed below are a general guide; always seek further advice if you are unsure.

Loans

Interest charged on a loan taken out for business purposes is normally a tax-deductible revenue expense, whereas any repayment of the capital amount itself is not.

Leases and hire purchase

If business assets such as equipment are leased or rented, so that you never actually own them, the full rental expense is normally allowable against tax. This remains true even if the rental amount reduces to a lower secondary figure after a fixed period. If the period when the 'full-price' rental is paid is actually significantly less than the likely useful life of the asset concerned then the tax inspector may want to make an adjustment, but a period of two to five years for equipment such as vehicles and computers should not cause a problem.

If the contract involves the purchase of the asset however, or gives the right to purchase the asset, such as applies under lease purchase arrangements, then the correct tax treatment is to treat the asset as if it had been owned from the outset. Payments made to the finance company under the contract are then a combination of loan repayments and interest charges.

Motor expenses

The area of tax allowances for vehicles is a particularly complex one and you may decide to consult a qualified accountant for advice on your specific situation. HM Revenue & Customs will permit a claim against tax for the proportion of total motor expenses that matches the proportion of business mileage to total mileage. Thus if total mileage is 10,000 per annum, and 8,000 miles of that total was for business travel, then 80% of total motor expenses could be claimed against tax. This is an area where all expenses should be recorded and entered onto the tax return and then an entry made for the amount disallowed, one-fifth in this particular example. The disallowed amount should be written in the box for disallowable expenses to show the tax inspector clearly that the non-business proportion of motor expenses has not been deducted against tax.

Remember this

The tax inspector can ask to see supporting evidence for your mileage calculations, and it is therefore very important to keep an accurate record or log of mileage, showing details of and the reasons for business trips.

Subscriptions

Membership fees for professional and trade bodies and Chambers of Commerce are normally allowable against tax. However, even if you find them useful for business purposes, HM Revenue & Customs will normally disallow costs such as sports and social club memberships.

Entertainment

Entertainment expenditure, except for staff entertainment, is not tax allowable at all. You may hear that it is allowable if you are entertaining foreign customers; this was once true but has long-since been abolished. The disallowance extends to 'business lunches', whether or not you really find lunch with your biggest customer or supplier more of an ordeal than a pleasure!

Entertaining of employees can be tax deductible up to a fixed amount each year; this does not have to be spent all in one go at Christmas despite the fact that the allowance is often referred to as the 'Christmas Party Allowance'.

Hotels and subsistence

Overnight stays away on business are tax allowable for accommodation and for the cost of meals. The rules can vary according to the nature of your business. Note that if you do not stay away overnight, you cannot normally claim the cost of meals, even for a business trip that takes all day and forces you to eat away from home.

Travel

Travel from your normal place of business to a customer is tax allowable, but note that travel from home to your place of business is not allowable. Disputes can arise with the tax inspector if a contract leads you to spend substantial periods at a client's own premises, and HM Revenue & Customs may seek to disallow the cost of travelling there from your home. Guidelines exist about the proportion of total time spent at a given client's premises which may trigger travel costs being disallowed. It would be wise if you are in this situation to take professional advice and avoid an unpleasant shock later.

Ensure also that you can demonstrate that your business is operated from home, and that you normally work from there, store equipment there, and that your accounting books and records are maintained there.

Allowable expenses

Here are a few more unusual expenses that may be tax allowable:

Newspapers and magazines may be allowable if they are used for business and research. Costs of computer magazines, for example, might fall into this category.

Special protective garments will generally be allowable as an expense.

If you use part of your home as an office then certain expenses of running the home may be tax allowable, but it may be simplest to estimate the expense by claiming a small fixed sum per week.

Grace Morris might claim against tax for (say) one-half of the rent, light, heat and other expenses of the whole property, since the shop premises are downstairs. She might actually argue for a higher percentage for certain costs on the grounds, for example, that the shop uses more light, heat and power than does the flat. Ben Martin would be unwise to try to claim more than a couple of pounds per week, since he spends most of his working time away from home. However, he writes up his books and records there, keeps his taxi in the garage overnight, and sometimes works on it at weekends, so a small claim would be in order. Hardip Singh uses his spare bedroom as an office, and his garage is used to store building materials, and so a claim against tax for some of his domestic running costs would be justified.

Remember this

Be careful, however, about claiming part of your mortgage interest (if you have one). While this might be allowable it can make you liable for some tax on your house when you sell it – get advice if you are thinking of claiming this.

Simplified Expenses Scheme Rules

The rules described in this chapter so far apply in most cases for most businesses. However, since April 2013 you have been able to do your tax accounting using a different set of expense rules – referred to as the Simplified Expenses Scheme. For some expenses it is now allowable when reporting these expenses incurred on your tax return to use a simplified approach.

This includes allowing 'flat rate' deductions for motor expenses. For example, instead of listing fuel and servicing or repairs costs as they are incurred, you simply report how many business miles are driven at a fixed cost – at the time of writing this is 45p/mile for the first 10,000 miles driven on business in the year and 25p/mile for business miles driven beyond this level.

Similarly if you use your house as an office you can charge a flat rate rather than have to compute the 'wholly and exclusive' cost by allocating your household bills between private and business use. The flat rates allowed at the time of writing are based on how many hours your home is used for business purposes each month as follow:

- 25–50 hours/month £10
- 51–100 hours/month £18
- 101+ hours/month £26

These costs are only applicable for your tax return however, and the rules explained before this section on how to include actual costs in your business accounts must be used normally or your cash book will not balance with your bank account statement.

Focus points

- What you can deduct for tax purposes can be complicated so you may find it useful to speak to an accountant or other financial adviser to get details specific to your circumstances.
- Things to watch out for include:
  - costs incurred not entirely related to your business
  - costs of buying capital items
  - loan repayments
  - lease and hire purchase costs
  - motoring costs where you are using your own vehicle for private and business use
  - subscriptions and membership fees
  - entertainment costs
  - hotels and subsistence
  - travel costs – from home to work or to visit clients
- If you wish to use the simplified expenses scheme for your tax return do beware you will need to record actual expenses incurred in the normal way in your cash book or it will not balance with your bank statement when you do a reconciliation.

Purchase of equipment

In this chapter you will learn:

▶ *How to record purchases of equipment*
▶ *How to calculate the capital allowances on equipment*
▶ *The special rules for purchasing cars*

You will know from the last chapter that capital expenditure is not tax deductible when spent in the way that revenue expenses are. However, the purchase of equipment such as computers, machinery and vehicles does get tax relief, under the system of 'capital allowances' that applies in the UK. This allows you to deduct part, or often all, of any capital expenditure for each year you own or use the asset.

In your annual personal tax return, those pages dealing with self-employment contain boxes enabling the calculation of the taxable profit figure before capital allowances, and then a separate set of boxes to deal with the capital allowances themselves.

The return does not include a working sheet for calculating capital allowances, however, and the tax return guide does not go into many details either. HM Revenue & Customs website does give an explanation of how to do the calculations and provides some examples.

This chapter looks at the process of recording the purchase of items of capital equipment and then calculating the capital allowances on them. It covers business plant and machinery and the special rules for motor cars. However, the subject of capital allowances is a complicated one, and can only be covered in outline here. If you do use an accountant to prepare your final accounts and tax return, then simply follow the instructions set out below in the first three paragraphs of the section on recording transactions. If you do not use an accountant, read through this chapter and HM Revenue & Customs guidance very carefully. Your local Tax Enquiry Centre can also help; it is possible for you to visit with your books and records, and to work through the figures with a member of staff.

Recording transactions

Outright purchases of equipment are simple to record. The amount paid is shown in the 'Total' column, and then also included in the 'Purchase of equipment' column. When equipment is rented, that is to say when there exists no right to purchase it, the cost is simply treated as a business expense, and included under other finance charges, or under motor expenses if it relates to a vehicle.

Equipment may also be acquired in instalments, through a hire purchase or lease purchase arrangement; or a loan may be taken out to finance the purchase. These types of transactions are more complicated to handle. If you use the services of an accountant it may be easiest simply to include the payments in the 'Purchase of equipment' column and let the accountant sort them out. However, if you are handling your own affairs, you will have to make the necessary adjustments.

One way to deal with these, although unorthodox in accounting terms, is to record two contra entries: the first being the purchase of the asset for the full cash price; the other as capital introduced into the business. These entries record that you as the business owner have put the money into the business in order to buy the asset. The fact that you were able to do so by borrowing the money does not change things. As a result, the capital repayments each month or quarter can then be posted under 'Drawings'. The interest element goes to other finance charges, and will be an allowable expense for tax purposes.

Remember this

Working out the split of a monthly payment between capital and interest is complex, and you should get the help of the lender to do this for you when you take out the finance. Failing that, a rough approach is to divide the total amount of capital borrowed by the number of payments to be made, and treat the result each month as the capital element and the rest as the interest charges. This method will, however, understate the true interest charge in the early years and overstate it in later years.

EXAMPLE

Grace Morris buys a new freezer for the shop for £3,000, and will pay for it in 12 instalments of £300 each. Because it is a short credit agreement, she decides to use the simple calculation method above to decide how much of each payment is capital and how much is interest.

$$£3,000 \div 12 = £250$$

Therefore £250 of each monthly £300 payment is capital, that is to say repayment of the original sum borrowed, and the balance of £50 is interest charged.

Figure 9.1 shows two entries in Mrs Morris's cashbook. The first is the entry for the initial purchase and the loan. There is no cheque number, because she has not had to pay out the £3,000 as she has arranged finance for it. The £3,000 expenditure is, therefore, a contra entry with a similar entry shown in receipts as capital introduced. The subject of capital introduced is dealt with in more detail in Chapter 15. The net effect is to leave the bank balance itself unchanged, as indeed it should be since no money has actually gone out of the business at this point, and the acquisition of the freezer at the purchase price of £3,000 is now reflected in the books.

The second entry is that needed for each of the 12 monthly payments of £300. Following the calculation above, £250 is posted into the drawings column and the remaining £50 is recorded as an interest payment.

Capital introduced is, in fact, simply the opposite of drawings; it is money put into the business rather than money taken out. Just as the initial loan was shown as capital introduced, the repayments are recorded as drawings. Figure 9.2 shows in summary form all entries connected with the purchase of the freezer, the initial contra entries and then the 12 monthly payments, reflecting the actual payments out of the bank account. The totals at the bottom of the analysis show the sum of £3,000 for purchase of equipment, which correctly records the cash price of the freezer, plus £600 of interest charges, which is the total interest suffered. Total payments are thus (£300 × 12) £3,600. Finally there are two total entries for £3,000, one under drawings and one under capital introduced. These entries are needed to record that Mrs Morris withdrew £3,000 from the business, having previously injected £3,000 into it. The two

Date	Payments out	Total	Equipment	Drawings	Finance	Date	Payments in	Total	Capital int.
1 1X	Freezer (paid by loan)	3,000.00	3,000.00			1 1X	Contra for freezer loan	3,000.00	3,000.00
Mth 1	Repayment	300.00		250.00	50.00				

Figure 9.1 Grace Morris – purchase of freezer.

Date	Payments out	Total	Equipment	Drawings	Finance	Date	Payments in	Total	Capital int.
1 1X	Freezer (paid by loan)	3,000.00	3,000.00			1 1X	Contra for freezer loan	3,000.00	3,000.00
Mth 1	Repayment	300.00		250.00	50.00				
Mth 2	Repayment	300.00		250.00	50.00				
Mth 3	Repayment	300.00		250.00	50.00				
Mth 4	Repayment	300.00		250.00	50.00				
Mth 5	Repayment	300.00		250.00	50.00				
Mth 6	Repayment	300.00		250.00	50.00				
Mth 7	Repayment	300.00		250.00	50.00				
Mth 8	Repayment	300.00		250.00	50.00				
Mth 9	Repayment	300.00		250.00	50.00				
Mth 10	Repayment	300.00		250.00	50.00				
Mth 11	Repayment	300.00		250.00	50.00				
Mth 12	Repayment	300.00		250.00	50.00				
TOTAL		6,600.00	3,000.00	3,000.00	600.00			3,000.00	3,000.00

Figure 9.2 Grace Morris – purchase of freezer.

amounts offset each other, and therefore have no net effect on the accounts.

Under the system in this book any receipts from the sale of equipment are simply recorded as a negative expense, subtracted from the figures on the payments side of the book. Appendix 4 provides a more detailed explanation.

Capital allowance calculations

The rules for calculating capital allowances can vary from year to year, with the Chancellor of the Exchequer changing the percentages and details of special allowances that might apply for the next year in his annual budgets. The examples below use a 18% rate – this is the rate that applies at the time of writing.

At the end of the year the total of the 'Purchase of equipment' column gives the capital cost of all equipment acquired in the year, even if some of it may not have been paid for in full. There are special rules for what capital allowances can be claimed in years you buy equipment for use in your business. Currently you can usually spend up to £25,000 on business equipment and get 100% of this as a capital allowance in the year of purchase. This is called the Annual Investment Allowance (or AIA). This allowance is likely to cover much, if not all, of your capital purchases in a year *as a small business*. If it doesn't cover it all, you can still probably claim a capital allowance of 40% in the year you bought the equipment (called First Year Allowances or FYA).

In the second or subsequent years of a business, anything of your equipment purchase cost still left without an allowance being received for it in the first year is added to the balance of what is called in accountancy jargon the pool of 'unrelieved expenditure' from earlier years, see below. Subtract from this new pool total any amount received in the year from the sale of equipment. Finally calculate 18% of the remaining balance to give the 'writing down allowance', which is the total capital allowance available to claim that year against tax for the purchase of plant and equipment. This figure is entered onto the tax return. The remaining balance now becomes the pool of unrelieved expenditure to be carried forward into the following year's calculation.

EXAMPLE

Hardip Singh started the year with a pool of unrelieved expenditure on equipment totalling £8,600. During the year he bought a cement mixer for £300 and a trailer for £100. He sold a van for £1,000. Figure 9.3 shows how he calculates the capital allowances available on the pool. The capital allowances to be entered into his tax return total £1,768 and the pool total for the next year therefore is £6,232.

	Pool	Allowances
Brought forward	8600	
Purchases (all AIA)		400
Sales	(1000)	
	——	
	7600	
Capital allowances @18%	(1368)	1368
	——	——
Pool carried forward	6232	1768

Figure 9.3 Hardip Singh – capital allowances.

The capital allowances treatment for motor cars is more complicated. They usually aren't allowed to be used for AIA or FYA purposes unfortunately. Cars are instead normally put directly into the normal 'pool' if their emissions rating is less than 130 g/km and get the same 18% allowances each year then as described above in Singh's example. If their emissions rating is more than this they go into a separate pool of their own (i.e. not with other equipment) and instead only get a 8% allowance each year. There are, however, some particular points to note.

▶ **Notes**

1 If a car is used privately as well as for business then keep this in its own pool and, after completing the capital allowances calculation for this asset by itself, a deduction of

an appropriate percentage is needed to reflect the private use element over the last year. The result is a capital allowances tax allowance that reflects only business use.

2 If a car is sold during the year, deduct the proceeds of the sale from the remaining pool balance for whichever pool it is in. If it is in its own pool (e.g. has private usage as per point 1 above perhaps) and the result of this deduction is a negative figure, then a so-called 'balancing charge' arises, to be included on your tax return. This increases the amount of taxable profits on which you have to pay tax. If, as is more normal, there still remains a balance of unrelieved expenditure, this is a balancing allowance, which has to be included on the tax return and reduces the amount of taxable profits.

3 Note that no capital allowances are due in a business where the owner claims a mileage rate for each business mile travelled rather than recording the motor expenses in full.

EXAMPLE

Grace Morris has an estate car which she bought some years ago. At the beginning of the present year the pool of cost on which capital allowances had not been claimed totalled £2,000. Although she uses the vehicle mainly for carrying goods from the Cash and Carry, it must be classified as a motor car for capital allowance purposes, because it was constructed for carrying passengers. During the year she sold the estate car for £1,000 and purchased a new one for £10,000 with emissions of 180 g/km. Her records showed that private mileage represented 10% of her total mileage for both her cars.

Figure 9.4 shows how the allowances are calculated. Both the old and new cars must have their own pool as there is private use of the vehicle to take into account (as per note 1 above). Also note that, for both the balancing allowance and the writing-down allowance on the new vehicle, the 10% private usage deduction is the last part of the calculation.

	Old car	New car	Allowances
Pool brought forward	2000		
Sale in year	(1000)		
Balancing allowance	(1000)		1000
Purchase		10000	
Writing-down allowance (8%)		(800)	800
10% private use			(200)
Pool c/f	—	9200	
Allowances given			1600

Figure 9.4 Grace Morris – capital allowances on car.

Focus points

For many small businesses now capital allowances can be ignored as the Annual Investment Allowance limit means you can just deduct them in your tax accounts like other purchases (i.e. you get 100% of the cost as an allowable expense).

However, handling the capital allowance calculations is sometimes complicated. If all else fails, a key point to bear in mind is that you need to be able to tell your accountant (if you use one), or HM Revenue & Customs about:

* any equipment acquired during the year and its cost
* any equipment sold during the year and the sales proceeds
* the interest element of any repayments you have made when assets are acquired under some type of credit agreement
* cars have their own special rules that aren't like other business equipment.

Credit cards

In this chapter you will learn:

- ► *How to use a credit card for business*
- ► *How to deal with business expenses charged to your credit card*
- ► *How to file your credit card transactions*

The details below explain how to deal with business expenses charged to your credit card. Note that any sales receipts by credit card should be handled as cheque receipts, and that the charges made to you by the credit card company should be included under other finance charges as an expense item.

How to use a credit card for business

In the same way as having a separate bank account for business purposes, it is helpful to have one or more credit or charge cards used solely for business expenditure. If both personal and business expenditure are paid on a single card, then some of the items paid on the credit card bill will need to be shown under drawings. If a card is used for both private and business costs it may not be possible to charge any interest against tax, and you will almost certainly not be able to charge any annual card fee against tax, since the expenditure will not be wholly for business purposes.

Remember this

It is a good idea to pay off a credit card balance in full every month if you are able to for the simple reason that interest charges on a credit card can be a lot higher than most other forms of finance.

Bill paid in full

Where a credit card bill is paid in full, recording that is simply a matter of entering the amount paid in the 'Total' column and then analysing the various categories of cost incurred into the appropriate analysis columns.

On the credit card statement, note each item according to the category of expenditure (cost of sales, motor expenses, stationery, and so on). If there are any private expenses, mark them as drawings. Then at the bottom of the bill, calculate subtotals for each of these categories, and just check that when the subtotals are added you do reach the same total as the 'Total' amount. These various subtotals are the figures to enter into the analysis columns.

EXAMPLE

Ben Martin's Visa statement records the following expenditure:

1 Two purchases of diesel from High Road garage.

2 Purchase of a cashbook and two lever-arch files.

3 Payment for a business advertisement in the local newspaper.

4 Print costs for some business cards.

5 A deposit for a family summer holiday.

Figure 10.1 shows how the statement appeared, and Ben's calculation of the subtotals. Figure 10.2 then shows how they were entered in the cashbook when he paid the Visa bill.

When only part of the bill is paid off

The correct way to handle this situation is to open a separate cashbook to record only credit card payments, and to show payments from the bank account as movements between the two accounts. This may be too complicated for a very small business, in which case use a similar approach to that for purchase of equipment on credit.

Enter transactions on the payments side of the cashbook exactly as if you had paid the bill off in full. Then, on the receipts side, enter a contra entry as 'capital introduced' for the amount not (yet) paid off. When in a subsequent month all or part of the remaining balance is paid off, enter the 'excess' payment over and above the amount charged to the card during that month as drawings.

EXAMPLE

The facts in Figure 10.3 are exactly as those in Figure 10.2, except that Ben Martin paid only £100 of the bill. The difference between the amount shown in the payments side and the contra entry on the receipts side of the cashbook is £100.

Next month he charges the following to his credit card.

1 Two more bills for fuel from the garage.

2 A subscription to *Black Taxi* magazine.

VISA

Mr B Martin
1 The Square
Histown
HH1 1HH

23.6.201X

26.5	High Road garage	*Cost of sales*	16.45
3.6	The Stationery Shop	*Admin.*	14.23
4.6	High Road garage	*Cost of sales*	19.56
5.6	The Histown Advertiser	*Advertising*	45.98
12.6	Pronto Printo	*Admin.*	32.56
18.6	Sunny Days Holiday Co	*Drawings*	90.00
TOTAL			218.78

Cost of sales	*Admin.*	*Advertising*	*Drawings*
16.45	14.23	45.98	90.00
19.56	32.56		
36.01	46.79	45.98	90.00

= £ 218.78

Paid in full 2/7

348

Figure 10.1 Ben Martin's Visa statement.

Date	Payments out	Ch. no.	Total	Cost of sales	Administration	Advertising	Drawings
2/7	Visa	348	218.78	36.01	46.79	45.98	90.00

Figure 10.2 Entry in Ben Martin's cashbook for Visa bill.

(Payments side)

Date	Payments out	Ch. no.	Total	Cost of sales	Administration	Advertising	Drawings
2/7	Visa	348	218.78	36.01	46.79	45.98	90.00

(Receipts side)

Date	Payments in	Total	Sales	Capital introduced
2/7	Visa (contra)	118.78		118.78

Figure 10.3 Entry in Ben Martin's cashbook for part payment of Visa bill.

At the end of that subsequent month Ben is able to pay off the whole of the balance. His bill and the calculations he makes on it are shown in Figure 10.4. The interest has all been shown

VISA

Mr B Martin
1 The Square
Histown
HH1 1HH

		23.7.201X
	Total from previous statement	218.78
3.7	Payment received – thank you	100.00
	Drawings	118.78
	Interest *Drawings*	1.25
25.6	High Road Garage *Cost of sales*	17.46
30.6	Taxicab publications *Admin.*	32.00
5.7	High Road Garage *Cost of sales*	14.53
TOTAL		184.02

Cost of sales	*Admin.*	*Drawings*
17.46	32.00	118.78
14.53		1.25
31.99	32.00	120.03

= £ 184.02

Paid in full 5/8

357

Figure 10.4 Ben Martin's second Visa statement.

under 'Drawings', although it would be possible to calculate the 'business' element and post that under finance charges. The balance brought forward (which is the same as the amount shown as capital introduced in last month's entry) is treated as drawings.

Figure 10.5 repeats the cashbook entry shown in Figure 10.3, then shows the entry for the following month. The figures have been totalled, and the amount shown as capital introduced has been deducted from drawings. If you compare this with the transactions for the two months you will find that all are now accurately recorded. The figure for drawings, in particular, is made up of the deposit on the family holiday and the interest charge.

Filing

Invoices and receipts slips for credit card purchases should be kept separately. You could perhaps punch holes in an A4 envelope to hold them and keep this at the front of the lever-arch folder. When the credit card statement arrives check the invoices and receipts against it, then staple them to the back of the statement. The cheque number and date of payment should be written on the front of the credit card statement before it is filed in the usual way, and the amount of the payment (or 'paid in full') should be written on the front of the statement as well.

Notes on timing

Paying for something by credit card is really the same as paying for it by cash, debit card or cheque. Strictly speaking, the expense is incurred on the day that you use the card. The system in this book, however, records the expense only when the credit card bill is paid. Generally this will not cause a problem, but be careful of the following situations:

1 **If you miss a payment completely.** Most credit and charge cards require a minimum payment to be made each month, but if this is missed they will normally carry the balance forward to the next month, adding interest charges and in

(Payments side)

Date	Payments out	Ch. no.	Total	Cost of sales	Administration	Advertising	Drawings
2/7	Visa	348	218.78	36.01	46.79	45.98	90.00
5/8	Visa	357	184.02	31.99	32.00		120.03
TOTALS			402.80	68.00	78.79	45.98	210.03
Deduct capital introduced			118.78				118.78
			284.02				91.25

(Receipts side)

Date	Payments in	Total	Sales	Capital introduced
2/7	Visa (contra)	118.78		118.78

Figure 10.5 Entries in Ben Martin's cashbook after payment of second bill.

some cases a late payment charge. If you miss a payment, treat it as a bill that was not paid in full. Enter it on the payments side as if it had been paid in full, and then show the same amount on the receipts side as capital introduced.

2 **At the end of the year.** Expenses incurred during the last month of the financial year and charged to a credit card will not be paid until the new business year has started. Yet the expenses concerned would be correctly deducted against tax in the previous year. The solution is to make an adjustment for such amounts due as a 'creditor', and this will be covered in Chapter 21. Be careful to do this consistently; as well as increasing costs from card bills paid after the end of a business year, you must similarly reduce them for the bill paid and entered in the first month of the next year. In practice, provided the amounts are small compared to the total expenses of the business, it is unlikely that HM Revenue & Customs will raise an objection if you consistently record the expense as occurring in the month the bill is paid.

3 **At the end of a VAT quarter.** VAT is complex and is dealt with in more detail in Chapter 17, but the principle here is the same as that for the year end; you will obtain relief for what is called 'input' VAT suffered in the quarter when the credit card bill is paid, not the quarter in which the expense was incurred. Again, if you are going to make an adjustment you would have to do so consistently, in one period or the other, not in both. You should note that financial penalties can be raised by HM Revenue & Customs when VAT is under-declared. If you find that the net value of errors on previous VAT returns is more than £2,000 then you must advise your local VAT office of that fact. If, however, the error(s) total £2,000 or less then you can simply include the value of the adjustments on your next VAT return. Penalties are normally mitigated when the reason underlying the error is a reasonable one.

Focus points

* Used carefully, credit cards can be a useful way of managing your cashflow as a business as you can obtain goods and services when you need them, but delay payment until later – perhaps after a customer you have given credit to has settled their bill. However, you must be careful if you operate this way to ensure you avoid expensive interest charges, where possible, if you don't pay off the full credit card bill each month.

* Pay off credit card bills in full each month whenever possible, to avoid expensive interest charges.

* Treat any part payment in the same way as the purchases of equipment on credit.

* Make sure that the expense is correctly recorded if a payment is made.

* Make adjustments if needed for timing differences at the year end and at the quarter end if your business is VAT-registered.

Petty cash

In this chapter you will learn:

▶ *Two methods for dealing with petty cash*
▶ *The advantages and disadvantages of each method*

This book-keeping system starts from bank statements. Inevitably, however, you will pay some expenses in cash, such as items of stationery, taxi fares and so on. There are two ways to ensure that these items are correctly recorded, both based on the idea that you accumulate the cash receipts and from time to time write a cheque to cover the accumulated cost. That cheque is then treated in the same way as when paying off a credit card, by simply analysing the total payment across the relevant expenditure categories.

This chapter will show you how to be methodical about your petty cash.

Cheque reimbursement

The simplest approach is not to keep any sort of physical petty cash 'float' at all. When you need to pay cash you use your own money, but you must still keep the receipts carefully. Then, at (say) monthly intervals, sort those receipts into the categories of expenditure used in the cashbook. Probably most will be general administrative expenses and travel expenses. Use a separate sheet of paper and list out the receipts under each category before adding up the amounts to get to separate subtotals. Add the subtotals to get the total for which the cheque is made out. Post the subtotals into the cashbook against the overall cheque total, and pay the cheque into your personal bank account.

EXAMPLE

Ben Martin has receipts for a map, some de-icer, accommodation following a long trip when he could not get back that night, a pen and a book of stamps. Figure 11.1 shows how he wrote these up on a sheet of paper, and Figure 11.2 shows how he entered them into his cashbook. He paid the cheque into his own personal bank account.

```
Motor Expenses:
7/5        De-icer                              3.49
1/6        Mapbook                              4.99
                                                8.48

Administration Expenses
28/6       Pen                                  1.19
28/6       Stamps                               2.60
                                                3.79

Travel Expenses
2/5        Clearview B + B, Hastings            23.00

Total                                           35.27

Ch. no.  362  10.7
```

Figure 11.1 Ben Martin's petty cash list.

Date	Payments out	Cheque no.	Total	Cost of sales	Motor exes.	Admin	Travel
10.7	Petty cash	362	35.27		8.48	3.79	23.00

Figure 11.2 Ben Martin's cashbook record of petty cash.

ADVANTAGES AND DISADVANTAGES

An advantage of this method is its informality, but for that very reason it is easy, over the weeks, to lose receipts or forget what they were for. If you spend a lot of cash the method may soon become unwieldy. Perhaps most importantly of all, if you do not get a receipt, you may not remember to claim for reimbursement of the cost. This might be problematic for a business like Mr Martin's, as he may make many cash payments, for parking meters, toll fees for bridges, and so on.

Imprest petty cash system

The second method is to keep a petty cash tin, and to keep a certain cash float in it, say £100. Whenever you have paid for something in cash, put the receipt into the box and take out the amount of cash spent. If you do not have the receipt then write out a slip which explains what the payment is for. Printed petty cash slips are sold at stationers, although there is no reason why you cannot just use scrap paper for this. When the amount of cash in the tin gets low, cash a cheque or withdraw cash on your debit card to top up the petty cash back to the original balance of £100.

This method for petty cash is common and is known as the imprest system. Imprest is simply an archaic word meaning a loan.

EXAMPLE

Hardip Singh operates an imprest petty cash system, with a float of £300 in the petty cash tin. Whenever he pays for something in cash, he puts the receipt or a petty cash voucher for it into the cash tin and takes out the corresponding amount of cash. At the end of each week he checks that it balances. With an imprest system, the total of the cash remaining in the tin plus the total amount shown by the receipts should always equal the fixed float amount, £300 in this case. Whenever the balance falls below £100 Mr Singh writes up the petty cash receipts and then writes a cheque to bring the total in the tin back up to £300.

Figure 11.3 shows the calculations. However, while there was only £90 in the tin, the receipts totalled only £205 and Mr Singh does not know what happened to the missing £5. Since he cannot show what business expense the missing £5 was used for, he treats it as drawings. The entries made in his cashbook are shown in Figure 11.4.

```
Cost of Sales
1.9       Homeways Hardware                    35.00
10.9      Homeways Hardware                    10.00
12.9      Rubbish clearance                    40.00
                                               85.00

 Motor Expenses
4.9       High St Garage                       25.00
3.10      Benfords Auto Accessories            35.00
                                               60.00

 Travel Expenses
12.9      2 nights B+B (castle view)           60.00
          Croydon
                                              _____
                                              205.00

Cash in box                                    90.00
                                              295.00

Drawings?                                       5.00
483 15/10 £210                                300.00
```

Figure 11.3 Hardip Singh's petty cash list.

ADVANTAGES AND DISADVANTAGES

The advantages of this system are hopefully self-evident. At any time, the receipts and the cash in the tin when added together should always equal the imprest amount. If this check is performed regularly there is a much better chance of remembering when and for what any missing amount was used.

The reimbursement cheque is for the same amount as the total of the receipts, and so it can be analysed easily into the cashbook.

An imprest petty cash system is simple and works well with the accounting system in this book.

Date	Payments out	Ch. no.	Total	Cost of sales	Motor exp.	Travel exp.	Drawings
15/10	Petty Cash	483	210.00	85.00	60.00	60.00	5.00

Figure 11.4 Hardip Singh's cashbook.

Focus points

* Petty cash is a useful way to manage small business costs. However, to ensure your books are kept correctly some thought should be given to how best to track small payments.

* Use an imprest petty cash system, topping up the petty cash float back to a pre-set level. If you do not do this then at least keep receipts for all cash items and then at intervals write yourself a cheque in reimbursement from the business account.

Receipts – filing

In this chapter you will learn:

▶ *How to file invoices and other paperwork to back up your accounting records*

▶ *Different systems for cash- or credit-based businesses*

Until now we have concentrated on how to record expenses. In the next three chapters we will look at receipts, and in general terms these are easier to record. While it is necessary to ensure that expenses are analysed correctly among a number of different categories, there are only a few reasons why funds would be paid into a business bank account, as we shall see.

This chapter considers the filing of invoices and other paperwork to provide backup for the accounting records, Chapter 13 then looks at the entries made in the bank paying-in book, and Chapter 14 explains how the cashbook should be completed.

Cash or credit?

Unlike the system for the filing of purchase invoices received, there are two different situations to consider when looking at receipts. The business may be one that is run primarily on credit, where sales invoices are raised but only paid by customers later. Alternatively, the business may be one where goods or services are usually paid for at the time of sale. Even if some of these receipts are in the form of customer cheques or by credit card, this is commonly referred to as a cash business. The recording considerations vary for each of these types of business.

In a credit-based business there are generally fewer (but larger) transactions. Hardip Singh might have 50 customers in a year, whereas Grace Morris might have that many in a day. Hardip's invoices are generally paid by client cheque, so that each individual payment can be entered onto a paying-in slip, and can be related back to the sales invoice. In a cash-based business, even if a few payments are made by cheque, it is unlikely that it will be viable or sensible to try and identify individual sales transactions separately. The usual approach is to use set points at which takings are totalled, generally each day at the close of business.

Credit-based business

The standard sales filing system needed by a credit-based business is similar to that used for purchases. A sales invoice will be raised for each job completed, possibly using a pre-numbered duplicate invoice book. Using a sheet of carbon paper, as each invoice is written out a duplicate copy is left in the book. Invoices can also be produced on a computer, of course, perhaps using a word processor template.

The two essentials for an invoicing system are that the invoices should be sequentially numbered and that a duplicate copy is kept. The numbering system helps to ensure that no invoice is lost, and to reassure HM Revenue & Customs that the likelihood of error or fraud is low. Duplicate copies also provide a system for chasing unpaid bills.

File the duplicate copies in the same way as bills paid. Use a separate lever-arch file with a divider card and file the invoices as yet unpaid above the divider card in issue order. When the invoice is finally paid write the date of payment on it and move it below the divider card. For most businesses it is sufficient to keep a file of the copy invoices in issue order.

Credit management

In addition to providing a record of business sales, invoices have an essential role to play in credit management. When looking at monies owed to you, you must encourage your customers to pay up promptly, and that includes following up debts with increasing vigour as they get older.

Invoices should state the time when they are due for payment: within seven days, two weeks or a month, rarely longer. You can issue a statement (i.e. summary of invoice(s) outstanding) before that time has expired, of course. Once the normal credit period has elapsed without payment being received, you may decide to send out a reminder that payment is overdue. If this does not result in payment you might, as the next stage, make personal contact by telephone.

While experience varies from business to business, most invoices get paid within 30 to 60 days of issue. An invoice outstanding for more than 90 days without good reason is often a trigger for enforcement action: either by instructing solicitors or a debt collection agency, or by personally taking out a court summons. This is neither expensive nor difficult, and a letter saying that such a summons will be issued without further warning if payment is not received in seven days may itself be a sufficient prompt to make the customer pay by return.

Debt chasing procedures require careful review of each situation, and a fine blend of tact and firmness when required. Make notes on the invoice duplicates to record what you have done to try to obtain payment, and when. Use this information to determine future credit arrangements for this customer – if you do repeated business with them – to ensure you aren't constantly chasing them for overdue debts.

EXAMPLE

Hardip Singh uses a pre-printed duplicate book for sales invoices, and has a similar one for issuing statements. He normally issues statements only when a payment is overdue, and gives people 14 days to pay. In practice he finds most people pay between four and six weeks after he bills them.

On 1 August he writes out an invoice for the latest job, billing Mr Davis £400 for roofing work. Having written this out and put the top copy in an envelope to be posted to Mr Davis, he looks through the duplicates. Two of the latest invoices are unpaid, but are still quite recent. An invoice for Mr Matthews is dated 7 July and still has not been paid, so he writes out a statement and posts it, noting on the duplicate that he has done so. Going further back through the book, all the other bills have been paid except for one to Mrs Jones, dated 14 June. A statement had been sent to her on 10 July. Mr Singh then rings Mrs Jones to remind her that payment of the bill is now long overdue, and is promised that the cheque will be in the post the following morning. He notes this on the copy invoice, and puts a note in his desk diary for two days' time to ring her again if a cheque has still not been received. See Figure 12.1 for copies of all these invoices as they appear after he has finished.

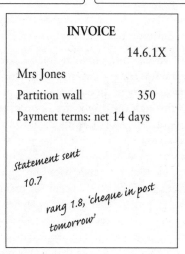

Figure 12.1 Hardip Singh's invoices.

Cash businesses

As noted earlier, never take cash from the till without leaving a note that this has been done, so that it can either be repaid later or accounted for. This is one of the most common reasons for cash businesses under-declaring profits, either deliberately or by accident, and questions in this area will often be raised during a tax investigation.

Using an electronic till will provide printed sales totals each day for the cash, cheques and credit card receipts that should be in the till, and this could be an ideal solution for Grace Morris. A useful method of cash control and record-keeping is to file these till records stapled to a sheet of A4 paper, then write on the same sheet a cash reconciliation of what was in the till, split into the different types of notes and coins, cheques and credit card receipts. Deduct any cash float that the till started with. This reconciliation should balance, or identify any 'unders' or 'overs'. If discrepancies are infrequent and small, and vary both under and over, you should have no problem with HM Revenue & Customs.

Ben Martin does not use a till because of the nature of his business, but uses a cash bag instead. He makes a point of not taking out any cash until he has totalled his takings at the end of each day. He then records takings in a cashbook which he keeps in the bag. He takes out his drawings, as explained in Chapter 3, and puts the rest of the cash to one side in a separate container, ready to be banked the following morning.

Focus points

* Use a system of sequentially pre-numbered invoices.
* Create a system to file invoices so you can easily track paid and unpaid invoices to chase debts as they become due.
* Check outstanding debts regularly and chase promptly when overdue.
* Never take cash from a till without leaving a note of how much and what for; ideally don't take cash from the till at all.

Receipts – paying-in book

In this chapter you will learn:

▶ *How to fill in your paying-in book*
▶ *How to file your paying-in slips*
▶ *How to fill in paying-in books for cash- and credit-based businesses*

The key aim when filling in the bank paying-in book is to link the supporting information on the sales file (Chapter 12) with the bank statements and the cashbook (Chapter 14). This should be in sufficient detail that if any one of them were lost it would be possible to recreate the records from the others.

The point made in Chapter 2 is repeated here: try to avoid using loose paying-in slips to bank business income. Use the slips in the paying-in book, so that there is less chance of losing them. The suggestions made in Chapter 6 about how to keep cheque stubs apply equally to your paying-in book stubs: bundle them together with an elastic band, and use a box file to keep them with the other records for the accounting year.

There are differences in how the paying-in book is filled in, depending on whether the business is a credit business or a cash business.

Remember this

Banks offer customers different types of paying-in books that are laid out in different formats. Speak to your bank to find the one that suits your needs best.

Credit business

The aim is to reference the paying-in slip back to the invoices, so that it is possible to check that the receipts for all the sales invoices have gone into the bank account.

EXAMPLE

Refer back to the receipts of Hardip Singh in the example in Chapter 3, Figure 3.3. He made two deposits during the month: on 10 June he paid in a cheque for £396.75, and on 20 June he paid in three cheques that totalled £2,750. Figure 13.1 shows both the front and the back of each counterfoil (stub) for the paying-in slips concerned, numbers 6000132 and 6000133.

Mr Singh must remember to record the invoice numbers, which means that in practice the paying-in slip should be filled in before the visit to the bank, since otherwise he will not have the

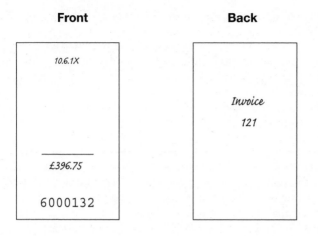

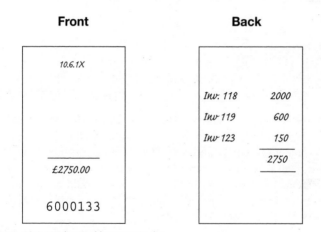

Figure 13.1 Hardip Singh's paying-in slips.

necessary information to hand. If he cannot do this, he should at least fill in the amounts of the individual cheques being banked on the back of the counterfoil, so sales invoice numbers can be added when he is next in his office. Other information would be available from the bank statement or the cashbook but picking up the invoice numbers themselves is a lot more difficult, particularly when several cheques are banked using a single paying-in slip.

Cash business

For a cash business, the important thing is to match up the paying-in counterfoil (stub) to the record of takings. This should not be a problem if takings are banked daily; however, if more than one day's takings are banked together then it is a good idea to prepare a reconciliation on the front of the last relevant takings sheet.

You should be aware that from a tax perspective, the more checkable evidence that can be provided to support the accounting records, the better. Fill in the counterfoils with the separate amounts for each type of note and coin, corresponding to the analysis that you have on the daily takings sheet. This in itself might not have prevented a person from taking cash out of a till before 'cashing up', but it all helps to show a well-controlled process.

EXAMPLE

Grace Morris cashes up her takings for 3 May. She has an electronic till listing which shows total takings as £342.56, stapled to a sheet of A4 paper to provide her daily takings record.

On the A4 sheet, as shown in Figure 13.2, Mrs Morris records the takings in the total amounts of cash for each individual denomination of note and coin. She produces a subtotal for cash, then lists the cheques and totals those. She does not accept payments by credit card, but if she did they would be treated in a similar way to cheques. The subtotals are then added together to get the grand total for that day.

The total in the till, after taking out £20 which is kept as a float each day, comes to £345.56, so she notes on the takings record that the till is £3 'over'. She does not take this £3 out, but records it as additional takings. If the till had been £3 under she would have recorded the takings for the day as £339.56. Her takings, her sales, for that day is the amount in the till. It is likely that there will be occasional mistakes resulting in there being more or less cash in the till than that shown on the till roll listing; the important point is that there is not a pattern of consistent and significant under-recording which suggests something other than accidental activity is occurring and should be checked.

£50	–
£20	100
£10	50
£5	55
£1	38
50p	6.50
20p	8.60
10p	5.30
5p	2.25
2p	1.46
1p	1.17
	268.28
Less float	20.00
TOTAL CASH TAKINGS	248.28
Cheques	14.32
	17.26
	23.43
	10.18
	32.09
TOTAL CQ. TAKINGS	97.28
TOTAL TAKINGS	345.56
Till list	342.56
	3.00 over

Figure 13.2 Grace Morris's takings list.

Grace Morris transfers the analysis to the counterfoil. This is in detail for cash, and in summary for cheques. She bags up the coins and the notes and deposits them at the bank. If there are any discrepancies arising when she banks the takings, because she miscounted for example, she would amend the counterfoil. When back at the shop she would make a note on the daily till listing of the change.

Focus points

* The above may seem straightforward – and often is if you follow careful rules about completing paying-in slips.
* However, very often business paying-in books record only totals paid in, and/or list cheques with no cross-reference to show how they relate to the sales invoices. The more you get into the habit of keeping full records, as above, the easier you make things at the year end. If you do use an accountant, then professional time saved should result in lower costs.

Receipts – cashbook

In this chapter you will learn:

▶ *How to complete the cashbook headings for receipts*
▶ *How to complete the 'narrative' column*

Once the necessary supporting information has been recorded, the final step is to enter transactions in the cashbook. Until now the cashbook has had only the payments side completed with headings. A similar but simpler procedure is now needed for receipts in the other columns of the cashbook.

Cashbook headings

Using the 32-column analysis book recommended earlier, now begin the receipts analysis at column 22. Head this up as 'Date'. Above the next three columns, 23–25, write the heading 'Payments in' – you will treat these as a single column, using it to record narrative explaining what the payment was for. The narrative will often simply be 'Cash/cheques'.

The next column, 26, should be headed 'Reference', using it for the reference number on the paying-in slip, if there is one. The next column should be headed 'Total', but leave the following column, 28, blank. It will be used for the same purpose as the column left blank on the payments side. Column 29 should be headed 'Income', and column 30 'Capital introduced'.

Using the receipts columns

With the possible exception of the 'Capital introduced' column, it may by now be fairly obvious how the various columns are used.

EXAMPLE

Figure 14.1 shows the entries made by Hardip Singh, completing the cashbook for the information provided in Chapter 3, Figure 3.3.

▶ **Notes**

1 The same basic rule for completing the receipts analysis applies as that for payments. The total is written in the 'Total' column, and the entries in the analysis columns for each line must together add up to that amount. In practice,

Date	Payments in			Ref.	Total		Income	Cap. Int.
22	23	24	25	26	27	28	29	30
10.6	Cheques			132	396.75			396.75
20.6	Cheques			133	2750.00			2750.00

Figure 14.1 Hardip Singh's cashbook – receipts side.

unless VAT is involved, the analysis will almost invariably be under the 'Income' column.

2 You may wish to analyse sales income over more than one column for your own information. If, for example, there are two or more distinct sides to your business, and you can easily distinguish between receipts for each, then it may be worth recording extra information to help with calculations of which are making the most profit. Grace Morris, for example, might want to set up the shop's electronic till by using different sales 'codes' to record the various stock lines that she sells, separating newspapers and magazines from food sales, for example. To make the best use of this information it would also be necessary to split the recording for cost of sales as well, to enable each category of sales to be set against the cost of sales for that category, and to thus produce what accountants would call the 'gross profit' for each.

EXAMPLE

Figure 14.2 shows Ben Martin's cashbook written up for receipts in the first week of May. These are the amounts first seen in Figure 3.5.

| Date | Payments in | | | Ref. | Total | | Income | Cap. Int. |
22	23	24	25	26	27	28	29	30
1.5	Balance b/f				2496.92	2496.92		
3.5	Cash				116.67		116.67	
4.5	Cash				68.56		68.56	
5.5	Cash				94.63		94.63	
6.5	Cash				72.49		72.49	
7.5	Cash				80.60	*3079.87* *793.80*	80.60	
	Cash contra				150.00	*= 2286.07*	150.00	

Figure 14.2 Ben Martin's cashbook – receipts side.

▶ **Notes**

1 Ben Martin started with a credit balance at the bank rather than an overdraft, and therefore the balance of £2,496.92 as at 1 May has to be brought into account. In exactly the same way that a starting overdraft was brought in on the payments side, the starting credit balance is brought in at this point on the receipts side. It is entered in the 'Total' column, and then written again in the blank column next to it (column 28).

2 Ben Martin writes up his records as he goes along, from information written by him on the cheque stubs and paying-in books. Transactions shown here cover only one week, and so Ben is not yet ready to total the columns at the bottom. Note that if he did do so, the totals would correctly cross-total back to the total of the 'Total' column. It is, of course, very useful to Mr Martin to know what the business bank account balance is. At the end of every week he therefore adds the total in the 'Receipts' column, including the balance brought forward, and notes the new balance in pencil, before adding the 'Total Expenses' column. Subtracting one from the other provides him with the revised bank account balance.

3   At present the sum of the 'Payments in total' column
    is £3,079.87 and that of the 'Payments out' column is
    £793.80, giving a net revised balance in the bank account of
    £2,286.07. If you check back you will see that these figures
    are the same as those included in the simple cashbook in
    Chapter 3, the totals columns of both the receipts (payments
    in) and payments out are as shown in the simple cashbook.
    The analysed cashbook has simply provided necessary
    analysis columns.

Narrative

A narrative in column 23 may seem slightly redundant on
this side of the cashbook, since at first sight it records only
that cash and cheques were deposited. However, here are a
few examples of different narratives that may occasionally be
needed.

Direct bank transfers. If a customer pays an invoice by a direct
transfer from their account then the receipt will appear on your
bank statement as a transfer from them. By definition there will
not be a paying-in slip for this receipt, and the sales invoice
number must be entered here for the invoice(s) paid off by the
direct bank transfer.

Interest paid. If your bank account pays interest on funds in
credit, a receipt entry for interest will sometimes be needed.

Standing orders. In some businesses customers may pay
by standing order. To get a standing order set up from a
customer, first get them to complete the details on a standard
standing order form, including a signature and date. It is
useful at this point to enter a reference on the form which
you ask the customer's paying bank to quote, so that you
can easily identify the customer when payments under the
standing order arrive. Photocopy the form for your own
record, then send the original to the customer's bank.
Payments should flow through automatically under the terms
of the standing order.

Capital introduced

In this chapter you will learn:

- ▶ *The basic principles of capital*
- ▶ *How to deal with more complex transactions*
- ▶ *Which items should not be treated as capital introduced*

Capital introduced into a business is the opposite of drawings. Whereas drawings are sums taken out of a business by its proprietor, capital introduced represents monies belonging to the proprietor that have been put into the business.

Simple introduction of capital

The most straightforward introduction of capital to a business is when a lump sum is paid into the business bank account. In that situation, the narrative describes where the money came from, and the analysis goes under 'Capital introduced'.

EXAMPLE

Hardip Singh sold some shares for £5,000, and paid the proceeds into the business account in order to reduce the overdraft. Figure 15.1 shows how the entry is recorded.

Date	Payments in			Ref.	Total		Income	Cap. Int.
22	23	24	25	26	27	28	29	30
7.8	Cheque (BTshares)			154	5000			5000

Figure 15.1 Hardip Singh – capital introduced.

▶ **Note**

It is important to record a clear explanation of where any capital introduced came from. The risk is that at a later stage HM Revenue & Customs may try to suggest that it came from business takings which had not been declared and which had been kept hidden.

More complex transactions

Two transactions that needed to be accounted for as capital introduced arose in earlier chapters: the purchase of equipment on credit and the part payment of a credit card bill. Refer back to Chapters 9 and 10 to refresh your memory. All funds coming into the business which are not business income are treated in this system as capital introduced. Set out below are some other examples.

Loans

In this system, any injection of funds into a business must be recorded as capital introduced, and any repayments recorded as drawings. The payment of the interest charges will be an expense.

EXAMPLE 1

The facts in Figure 15.2 are the same as those in Figure 15.1 above, except that the £5,000 injected into the bank account this time came from a loan taken out by Mr Singh in order to consolidate his overdraft. He has to repay the new loan at £200 each month, of which he calculates that £150 is capital repayment of the loan itself and £50 is interest charges.

The entries below show the initial payment into the business account of the £5,000 borrowed, and the first repayment.

Date	Payments out	Ref.	Total	Interest	Drawings
7.9	Transfer (loan rept.)		200.00	50.00	150.00

Date	Payments in	Ref.	Total	Cap. Int.	
7.8	Transfer (loan)		5000.00	5000.00	

Figure 15.2 Hardip Singh – loan and repayment.

EXAMPLE 2

In Figure 15.3, Mr Singh has again borrowed £5,000, but the loan repayments are now irregular. He makes three payments, one of £100, one of £300, and another of £250. Interest of £200 is then charged on the loan.

Date	Payments out	Ref.	Total		Interest	Drawings
7.9	Transfer (loan rept.)		100.00			100.00
7.10	Transfer (loan rept.)		300.00			300.00
7.11	Transfer (loan rept.)		250.00			250.00
30.11	Loan interest contra		200.00		200.00	

Date	Payments in	Ref.	Total		Cap. Int.	
7.8	Transfer (loan)		5000.00		5000.00	
30.11	Loan interest contra		200.00		200.00	

Figure 15.3 Hardip Singh – irregular loan repayment.

Follow these entries carefully. The first entry on the receipts side shows £5,000 coming into the business account, and being treated as capital introduced. The three payment entries show the payments going out of the account, and being treated as drawings.

Interest of £200 has been suffered and this is added but not actually paid from the current account. The interest is a business expense but since it has not gone directly through the business bank account, at present it is not recorded. In order to record it, it is necessary to use a contra entry, so that the balance on the business bank account does not alter. On the payments side of the cashbook the amount is included under interest charges, but what about on the receipts side?

The opposite of drawings is capital introduced. So far all repayments of the loan have been treated as drawings, as if they were repayments of capital. In fact, £200 of the total repayment comprised interest charges. Therefore drawings need to be reduced by £200, and the easiest way to do that is to increase capital introduced by £200.

Equipment introduced

This area is much more straightforward, and again requires contra entries. On occasion the business owner may put assets directly into the business rather than cash. In that case each asset needs to be placed under the heading of purchase of equipment, but because the balance at the bank will not itself have changed, a contra entry will be needed. Since the overall position is exactly the same as if funds to buy the asset had been put into the business by the proprietor, and the asset then purchased from a third party, the transaction is recorded as if that had in fact happened. The owner will need to place a fair open-market value on the asset at the time of its introduction to the business.

EXAMPLE

Figure 15.4 shows the situation after Grace Morris had inherited an estate car worth £8,000. The amount to be entered for the transaction is £8,000; for tax purposes the asset must be shown at its market value at the time it was taken into the business. The introduction of the car is shown on the payments side of her cashbook as a contra item under

Date	Payments out	Ref.	Total	Equipment
1.9	Contra (car inherited)		8,000.00	8,000.00

Date	Payments in	Ref.	Total	Cap. Int.
1.9	Contra (car inherited)		8,000.00	8,000.00

Figure 15.4 Grace Morris – equipment introduced.

'Equipment purchased'. Note in passing that tax allowances (capital allowances) will be available on the car as explained in Chapter 9, even though Mrs Morris did not actually pay anything for it. On the receipts side of the cashbook the contra entry goes under 'Capital introduced'.

Items not treated as capital introduced

There are some entries that can be misleading. An example is if a direct debit against the account 'bounces' (is not paid because there are not enough funds in the account). This will be shown on the bank statement in the way set out in Figure 15.5. The debit to BT for £450 appears to have gone through when it was called for by BT's bank, but this made the account overdrawn. As there was no overdraft facility in place, the debit was not actually paid, and was subsequently credited back onto the bank statement.

		Debit	Credit	Balance
3.7	DD BT	450.00		-125.67
3.7	Unpaid direct debit		450.00	324.33

Figure 15.5 Unpaid direct debit.

The simplest treatment is to put a line through both entries on the bank statement and not record it at all; when you think about it, the transaction did not ever actually happen.

Focus points

* Putting money (capital) or equipment you already own into a business can occur at any point not just when it started.
* Capital introduced is treated as negative drawings.
* Treat loan repayments as drawings and enter loan interest using contra entries.
* Introduce long-term assets at market value, with a contra to drawings.

End of month procedures

In this chapter you will learn:

▶ *How to reconcile your transactions with your bank account*
▶ *How to total up each month's page and check it is accurate*
▶ *How to start a new page for the next month*

After all business accounting transactions have been entered into the analysed cashbook each month, they need to be reconciled to the bank account. The cashbook page must be checked and totalled and a new page started for the next month.

Reconciliation

The type of bank reconciliation depends upon the way that records are kept. For Hardip Singh, the reconciliation is an integral part of the process of completing his books, since he doesn't write them up until the bank statement is available for the month. He then spends time doing the book-keeping entries. Starting with the payments, he enters each transaction in turn from his bank statement into the cashbook, both in the 'Total' column and under the appropriate analysis column. He is able to get the information for the analysis from the cheque-book stub and/or the file of paid bills. During this process he places a tick on the bottom of the stub for each cheque that has cleared through the bank. After entering all the payments in this way he looks through the cheque-book to identify any cheques written before the end of the month but which have not yet passed through the bank account, and he lists these on the bank statement.

Mr Singh then adds each column, and checks that the totals of all the analysis columns add up to the same figure as does the 'Total' column itself. When he has confirmed that they do, he writes a letter 'T' at the bottom of the 'Total' column to show that he has checked it totals both ways – down the column and along the row. This process is repeated for the receipts side of the cashbook.

The final entry in the cashbook each month is to subtract the total of 'Payments out' from total receipts, including the balance brought forward (whichever side it was on). The result should be the same as the balance on the bank statement: positive if in credit and negative if overdrawn. This figure becomes the balance taken forward to the next page, where the headings are written in and the balance brought forward is entered for the next month. Note that some analysis books have shorter sheets for all pages other than the inside cover sheets, allowing the analysis column headings to be written once only.

The final version of Mr Singh's cashbook after it has been completed for June, using the earlier entries from Figure 4.1, is shown in Figure 16.1.

The monthly book-keeping is not quite finished yet. Mr Singh then goes through the paying-in book to see if any deposits made have not yet been credited on the business bank statement. If they were paid into the account in the few days before the end of the month they should appear on the next statement. He simply lists these missing credits on the front of the current statement.

Finally he adds any missing receipts and subtracts any missing cheque payments from the balance on the statement. This provides the true bank balance (or overdraft) at the statement date.

For Ben Martin, the process is different. He wrote up his accounting records as he went along, and now needs to reconcile them to the bank statement. Almost invariably there will be some further entries to put in. He starts with his bank statement and ticks off each individual item for transactions that match to the statement itself and in the blank column of the cashbook used for the carry forward figure. If he wants to be doubly careful, he can also tick them off against the cheque-book stubs and paying-in slips.

▶ Notes

1 Some early transactions on the bank statement may not be on the page for the current month in the cashbook. These will be cheques written and deposits made in the previous month but which did not clear the bank until the current month. Since Ben Martin writes up his cashbook at the time he makes payments and deposits, it is correct that they are recorded this way, but he does need to check them off against the items not ticked off on the previous cashbook page to ensure that all are correctly processed.

Bank account no 123 456 23 Sort code 22-22-22 June 201X

Date	Payments out	Cheque no/Debit card	Total	Cost of sales	Employees	Admin.	Motor/Travel	Advertising	Legal/Prof.	Finance	Drawings
1 Jun	Bal b/f		2,040.53	2,040.53							
3 Jun	s/o County Leasing		345.22				345.22				
8 Jun	High St Garage	Debit	28.34				28.34				
10 Jun	V G Browns		25.68			25.68					
12 Jun	s/o H Singh		500.00								500.00
14 Jun	Charges		42.30							42.30	
18 Jun	Anytown Courier	235	43.69					43.69			
18 Jun	Smarts	Debit	692.59	662.59							30.00
21 Jun	DD NICO		28.40								28.40
23 Jun	Jones Plumb.	237	254.00	254.00							
23 Jun	Post Office Limited	Debit	150.00				150.00				
28 Jun	Print Presto	238	82.38			82.38					
30 Jun	DD Magnificent Mutual		100.00								100.00
30 Jun	TOTALS		4333.13	2,040.53 / 916.59		108.06	523.56	43.69		42.30	658.40

Figure 16.1 Hardip Singh – end of month.

2   There may be transactions on the bank statement that have not yet been entered in the cashbook. Examples might be direct debits, any standing orders that Mr Martin neglected to enter, and bank charges and interest. These items will be entered into the cashbook now, using the date as shown on the bank statement, even though this means that the dates in the cashbook will be out of order.

3   There may also be transactions in the cashbook which have not been ticked off, including some from earlier months that could not be ticked off until the current statement was received. These should be written on the front of the bank statement, both payments and receipts. By adding the receipts and subtracting the payments from the balance carried forward on the bank statement, Mr Martin can calculate the true balance at the bank. For him this will be a meaningful figure, since he keeps his books up to date as he goes along, and thus the revised balance for the bank statement should be the same as the balance calculated in the analysed cashbook itself.

Finally Ben Martin can total his cashbook in the same way that Hardip Singh did, by totalling the analysis columns, checking that the column totals cross-check with the 'Total' column, and indicating that fact by writing a 'T'. When he takes the total of the payments away from that of the receipts, he should reach the same figure as the one that he calculated on the bank statement.

Errors

Errors will occur, although using a computer spreadsheet can be a useful way of minimizing these (this area is covered in Chapter 27).

When the cashbook totals do not agree, the first step is to add up the figures again, to see if an error was made in keying the numbers. If there is still a problem, calculate the difference between the total you have and the total you should be getting; sometimes the figure itself will give you a clue as to what it is.

For example, if in Hardip Singh's case there was a difference of £42.30 on the payments side, a quick glance down the 'Total' column would show that the problem was probably to do with the charges. Possibly these had not been entered in the 'Total' column, or they had not been entered in the charges analysis column, or they had been erroneously entered in two different analysis columns.

If that process does not locate the error, check whether the difference divides exactly by nine. If it does, there is a likelihood that a digit has been transposed when entered into either the 'Total' column or the analysis column. For example, Mr Singh might have entered the standing order to County Leasing as £345.22 in the 'Total' column, but transposed two digits and written '£435.22' in the 'Motor expenses' analysis column. The difference is £90, which is divisible by nine.

Remember this

If you transpose two adjacent digits in any number you will find that the difference between the two numbers is always exactly divisible by nine.

If the error remains, take a ruler and cross-check each individual entry with the calculator, ensuring that the amounts in the analysis columns always add up to the amount in the 'Total' column for each individual cashbook row. Also check that the total brought forward has been correctly entered in both the 'Total' column and the blank one next to it, and that it has been carried down to the correct total at the bottom of the page.

If the error is that the balance does not agree with the balance on the bank statement (as adjusted, if appropriate), again calculate what the difference is. If there is only a single error, the problem can probably be identified directly from the amount itself. If there is more than one error it will be necessary to look carefully and ensure that every entry on both the bank statement and the cashbook has either been ticked or properly adjusted for. If there is still a problem, it may be necessary to go through the whole ticking-off process again, this time using a cross-bar mark on the tick to show that the transaction has been checked again. It can be useful to do this in a different colour, red for example. It can also be helpful to use an add-list calculator with a printout, making it easy to check that all keyed-in entries have been entered correctly.

Remember this

Always start a new page for each new month. If there are still some lines remaining on the first page, add the totals for that page and check that they all agree. Carry these totals forward to the first row of the same headings on the new page, and then add up the totals again on this page to check that they agree. It is easy to make copying errors.

Whether you complete the cashbook in pencil or ink is a matter of choice. Correcting errors made in ink with white fluid can get messy, and it may well be better to use pencil, at least in the first few months until you are fully comfortable with the system.

Focus points

* Reconcile the cashbook to the bank statement regularly – at least monthly when the bank statement is issued.
* Cross-add the cashbook to check for errors.
* Identify and resolve errors, do not be tempted just to carry them forward as a 'difference'. They'll just become harder to resolve later.
* If the difference is divisible by 9 you are likely to have transposed numbers in your cashbook.

VAT

In this chapter you will learn:

▶ *The basics of how VAT works*
▶ *How to record VAT as part of the book-keeping system*
▶ *When it is necessary to register for VAT*

Although VAT will be suffered on many goods and services that a business purchases, this tax is just treated as part of the purchase price unless the business proprietor registers for VAT.

It is compulsory to register for VAT once sales of goods or services liable to VAT exceed the VAT registration limit. The latest registration threshold is available from HM Revenue & Customs. Once registered, the proprietor must charge VAT on all taxable supplies.

The operation of VAT can be complex, but a brief overview of how VAT works is given here in the context of accounting and book-keeping issues. The main purpose of this chapter is to show how VAT is recorded as part of the book-keeping system. For further information on the operation of VAT contact your local HM Revenue & Customs office or visit their website (www.hmrc.gov.uk).

Some businesses find VAT quite straightforward; for others it is more involved. If you are unsure, you may want to consult a qualified accountant to ensure that you are completely clear about the VAT implications of the business transactions you enter into. Someone like Grace Morris, where the shop makes some sales that are liable to VAT and some that are not, would be wise to consult an accountant initially.

Brief overview of VAT

The following is a brief overview of the concept behind and practical application of the Value Added Tax system. As its name suggests, the system computes the 'value that is added' by a business, which it measures by comparing the 'taxable inputs' of that business to its 'taxable outputs' and then applies the VAT rate to it (usually 20%). If a business had input costs of raw materials at £100 a tonne, and produced finished goods worth £300 a tonne, the value added would be £200 for each tonne of production sold. The VAT calculation is more complicated than that in reality, since other costs are involved in operating the business and thus adding the value. These might include costs of running the premises, such as power, and the hire costs of the machinery needed in the production process. All these costs must be included to determine the real value added.

Accounting for VAT involves calculating total VAT that has been charged on all sales ('taxable supplies' in VAT jargon) made in a given period, and subtracting the 'input' VAT suffered by the business during that same period on its costs. Once a quarter (for most businesses), a VAT return has to be completed showing the VAT charged on sales, subtracting the VAT suffered on services and goods purchased. The business is in effect acting for the UK Exchequer as a tax collector. When the business has calculated its liability, it sends HM Revenue & Customs a cheque for the amount due, or more rarely, a refund claim if the VAT suffered on costs (input tax) exceeds VAT charged on sales (output tax).

Note that the definitions of taxability for VAT have little to do with the definitions used for income tax set out earlier in this book. A VAT supply (sale) can be standard-rated, reduced-rated, zero-rated or exempt from VAT, depending on the exact nature of the supply concerned. For example, food in general is zero-rated. This means that a business selling food in effect charges VAT at zero per cent, i.e. does not have to charge VAT on its sales, but may recover the VAT it pays on its business purchases, an advantageous state of affairs. Newspapers and books are also zero-rated, although stationery, including analysis books, is standard-rated.

It appears, therefore, that Grace Morris may have a lot to gain from the VAT system, since her supplies are surely virtually all zero-rated. Unfortunately things are not so straightforward in reality. Confectionery, for example, is standard-rated and thus excluded from the general rule that 'food' is zero-rated.

Another category is that of VAT-exempt supplies. There is no need to add VAT to these supplies when they are made, but a business which makes only exempt supplies (a pensions adviser, for example) cannot recover the VAT charged by its suppliers, whereas a business making zero-rated supplies can do so, as noted above. Always take further advice if you are in any doubt.

Accounting principles

When a business is VAT-registered, there is a key concept to bear in mind. Since the business is in effect acting as a tax collector, the VAT that it charges on sales is not the business's money at all, and thus it is important you don't treat it as your income. Instead it is kept separate until the time comes to complete the VAT return. Similarly, for a VAT-registered business the true cost of anything is the net (VAT-exclusive) cost, and this is the amount to record as an expense or as the cost of equipment. VAT suffered must be considered as something separate from costs, reclaimable in due course when the VAT return is completed.

Date	Details	Total	Motor	Admin.	Drawings	Finance	Advertising	Cost of sales	VAT
3 Jun	s/o County Leasing	345.22	287.68						57.54
8 Jun	Card High St Garage	28.34	23.62						4.72
10 Jun	V G Browns	25.68	21.40						4.28
12 Jun	s/o H Singh	500.00			500.00				
14 Jun	Charges	42.30				42.30			
18 Jun	235 Anytown Courier	43.69					36.41		7.28
18 Jun	Card Smarts	692.59			30.00			552.16	110.43
21 Jun	DD NICO	28.40			28.40				
23 Jun	237 Jones Plumb.	254.00						211.67	42.33
23 Jun	Card Post Office Limited	150.00	150.00						
28 Jun	238 Print Presto	82.38		68.65					13.73
30 Jun	DD Magnificent Mutual	100.00			100.00				
30 Jun	TOTALS	2292.60	482.70	68.65	658.40	42.30	36.41	763.83	240.31

Figure 17.1 Hardip Singh – analysed payments for June, if VAT-registered.

Cashbook entries – payments

For a VAT-registered business, the way the VAT is recorded in the analysed cashbook is to add a separate column in the analysis, both for payments and for receipts. Figure 17.1 shows again the analysed payments for June for Hardip Singh, but this time on the basis that he is VAT-registered. Expenses with VAT on them have been further analysed, with VAT-exclusive amounts shown under the appropriate analysis columns and the VAT itself written in a separate column at the end. Sometimes the VAT column is placed after the 'Total' column.

▶ **Notes**

1 Equipment leasing costs are generally subject to VAT.

2 The van is used for business purposes and so VAT on fuel can be reclaimed, provided that Mr Singh remembers to obtain a VAT invoice from the garage as evidence. A VAT invoice must show the supplier's VAT registration number. The system for cars used partly for business and partly privately is more complicated; all of the VAT can be claimed on the fuel, but it is necessary to add a fixed amount to VAT charged on sales ('outputs') to represent the 'supply' to the proprietor of some of the fuel (i.e. for the private use element).

3 For costs over £30 a proper VAT invoice should be requested from suppliers. The amount of VAT (at 20%) can always be calculated by multiplying the VAT-inclusive price by 1/6.

4 Bank charges and interest are VAT-exempt items, as are vehicle road fund licences.

5 Care must be taken in dealing with the entry for the purchases from Smarts. The total purchases came to £692.59, but £30 of this was for private use and VAT can only be claimed back on business purchases. The £30 in drawings does not change, and 1/6 of the amount previously

under 'Cost of sales' is shown as the input VAT of £110.43 reclaimable only on the business items.

6 The 'VAT' column is treated like any other in the analysis; it is totalled and brought into the cross-check calculation to ensure that the total of the analysis columns equals the total of the 'Total' column. Totals under the other analysis columns have reduced to match the amount now shown under the 'VAT' column.

Cashbook entries – receipts

Figure 17.2 shows the receipts side of Mr Singh's cashbook for June. The VAT fraction, 1/6, of receipts is now treated as VAT. Although the costs of the purchases made have been reduced slightly by the ability of the business to reclaim VAT, this cost reduction is more than outweighed by the reduction in value of sales that now suffer VAT.

This 'loss' may not always be the case. If your business is a business-to-business one, and your customers are mainly VAT-registered businesses themselves, then you will be able to increase the sales price you charge in order to recover the VAT without it affecting your customers, since they can reclaim the VAT. You will still be able to recover the VAT charged on your costs.

Date	Payments in			Ref.	Total		Income	Cap Int.	VAT
22	23	24	25	26	27	28	29	30	
10.6	Cheques			132	396.75		330.67		66.08
20.6	Cheques			133	2750.00		2291.67		458.33
					3146.75		2622.34		524.41

Figure 17.2 Hardip Singh – analysed receipts for June if VAT-registered.

End of quarter

At regular intervals a VAT return must be made. Provided you are able to report on a cash basis (i.e. just compute your VAT due on what money you have received or paid out), which is the normal basis for smaller businesses (seek advice if you are unsure), you simply add up the VAT totals recorded in your cashbook for the period. This gives the total VAT on outputs (sales) for the period, and the total VAT on inputs (costs).

When the VAT payment is written in the cashbook, it can be included under the 'VAT' column for payments. As a result, if there were no further entries between the time when the quarter ended and when the VAT payment was made, the total in the payments 'VAT' column would now match the total in the receipts 'VAT' column. In practice, because a month is allowed for completing the return and making the payment, the normal position will be a balance permanently in favour of the 'Receipts' column because other transactions will have occurred in the meantime. This balance will increase as the end of the VAT period approaches, then drops back to a low figure when the payment is made out to HM Revenue & Customs.

If you think about the nature of this balance you will realize that it represents a loan to you from the Exchequer. VAT is something that you collect on behalf of the State, but because you only have to pay it over at intervals you get the use of the money until then (although it is best not to think of this money as yours, as explained earlier, so it is always available to pay over when the VAT sums are due).

Flat-rate scheme

In addition to the 'normal' VAT system just outlined, some businesses can compute their VAT due using a so-called flat-rate scheme. This scheme is for smaller businesses and was introduced in April 2002. It is open to businesses with taxable turnover up to £150,000. Rather than the normal detailed output tax less input tax calculation, it offers a simpler approach. Depending on the type of business, a flat percentage rate of VAT is applied to all the sales, without any allowance for inputs. The rate concerned depends on the business carried on, and ranges upwards from 4% (which applies to businesses selling food and children's clothing) up to 14.5% (the flat rate used for accountants, architects and IT consultants).

The flat-rate scheme is intended to be easier for many small businesses. However, if the business is unusual in the way it operates, or if it has a particularly high level of inputs, then the VAT burden may actually be higher than it would be under the traditional system. Again, get advice on whether this is better for your situation, or review HMRC's online information, in deciding if this simpler system is worth adopting for your business.

Focus points

✳ VAT is a simple tax in principle but can be a complex tax to apply in practice. Many smaller businesses will need help at least in setting up an accounting system process to include VAT correctly.

✳ Small businesses may not have to register for VAT so won't have to charge it to their customers. However, once registered all of your costs in effect become VAT free (saving you 20% therefore).

✳ The VAT amount (at 20%) within a VAT-inclusive cost figure can be found by multiplying it by 1/6.

✳ Once registered VAT should normally be charged on goods and services you sell unless these are listed as being exempt or zero-rated supplies.

✳ The flat-rate VAT scheme may be a simpler method to operate for many small businesses – but be careful this doesn't actually cost you more money than you save in having a simpler accounting system. Using the traditional way of computing VAT may actually produce a lower bill for you in some cases.

✳ If you do register for VAT remember to add an extra column in your cash book to record the sums you pay/collect so you have the necessary information to complete your quarterly tax return.

Wages

In this chapter you will learn:

▶ *How to deal with wages*
▶ *How to account for PAYE tax deducted and national insurance*
▶ *The business implications of employing someone for the first time*

This chapter is concerned with the entries needed in the accounting records to deal with wages, PAYE income tax deducted and national insurance contributions. Like VAT, this can be another quite complex area and this book can highlight only some of the main points.

Employed or self-employed?

Whether someone carrying out tasks for the business is employed or self-employed is a crucial question to address, because it affects the way that payments made to them must be treated. If there is any doubt at all you should seek guidance, and in any case Check out the HM Revenue & Customs webpages (see http://www.gov.uk/government/collections/employed-or-self-employed). Businesses in the construction industry should also look for the relevant parts of the HMRC website as rules for this industry differ from normal rules.

The question of whether or not a worker must be classified as an employee depends upon the facts of each case. Some of the key points that need to be considered are set out below.

▶ Do they work only for the business, or do they work for other businesses as well? The more they work only for a single business the more likely they are to be employees of that business.

▶ Do they provide their own tools and equipment? The provision of small tools may not make a lot of difference, and is even traditional in certain trades, but the provision of large items of equipment is an argument in favour of self-employed status.

▶ Are they obliged to turn up for work, and is the business obliged to give them work when they are there? If so, they are probably employees. If either the business or they themselves can decide they are not working on a given day that is a good indication that they may be self-employed.

▶ Are they obliged to make good any mistakes in their own time and at their own expense? That is what would be expected of someone who was self-employed.

► Are they permitted to send someone else instead of turning up themselves? This is known as 'substitution' and is a strong indicator of self-employed status.

► Are they paid sick pay and holiday pay, and do they receive any benefits in kind such as a company car or membership of a pension scheme? If so, they are probably employees.

No single one of the above points is a conclusive test by itself. Two or three taken together, however, may give a strong indication and in most cases the various factors will be looked at together to gain a picture of the working practices concerned, and thus the overall position.

Consequences of employee status

While this chapter is mainly concerned with the accounting implications of employee status, be aware that taking someone on as an employee has many legal consequences. They may gain rights against unfair dismissal, there will certainly be health and safety implications, you must take out employer's liability insurance and be responsible for checking their rights to work in the UK. The employer will probably also become liable for sickness pay and maternity/paternity leave.

However, from an accounting point of view, the main consequence is that, like VAT, the employer is again put into the position of acting as tax collector for the State, for the income tax and national insurance contributions that employees suffer on their earnings. Once an employee is taken on, HM Revenue & Customs must be notified and they will send a detailed 'Employment Pack', a set of instructions on how to make the tax deductions and how and when to pay them over.

The basic system is that a tax 'code number' is issued for each employee by HM Revenue & Customs, based upon their personal tax position. Using the tax tables supplied in the Employment Pack, the amount of an employee's earnings paid so far in the tax year, and the amount of tax already deducted during the year, is used to look up the amount of PAYE income tax to be deducted from the week's or month's pay. A similar, though simpler, calculation gives the amount of national insurance contributions (NICs) to be deducted. It is the net figure after making these deductions that is paid over to the employee.

If you visit the HM Revenue & Customs website (www.gov.uk/business-tax/paye) you will find that there is an online PAYE tax calculator available, if you prefer that. You will also find you can pay your PAYE obligation online – see the details also found on this web page.

EXAMPLE

In July Mr Singh started work on a larger job, which needed two manual labourers. In the past he might have taken these on as self-employed, but HM Revenue & Custom's advice is that they should be treated as employees, even though they will be temporary workers. Mr Singh obtains from each of them their tax code numbers and the copies of form P45 which they were given when they left their previous employers. Form P45 will give the figures for taxable pay and tax deducted to date during the current tax year.

At the end of the first week each employee had earned £300 in gross wages. Their tax code numbers and the tax tables inform Mr Singh as their employer that he must deduct £30 in tax from the first employee, £25 from the second. This difference will most likely be due to some tax allowance available to one but not the other or some payment being collected by the Government via their payroll. These allowances are reflected in the individual's tax code numbers.

National insurance deductions (NICs) have fewer complications, and each employee needs to have £15 deducted. Mr Singh thus pays the first employee £255 net of tax and NICs, and the second £265. Each must also be given a payslip detailing the tax and NICs deducted. Before any payment is made to either worker these details must be reported to HMRC under the PAYE scheme currently in operation called Real Time Information (RTI). Once this has been done Mr Singh can pay his employees.

In addition to this, as employer he also has a liability to pay Employer's NI contributions on their wages, which amount to a further £20 each per week per employee. He therefore writes out a total cheque for £125 to the tax authorities.

As a small business with low PAYE payments each week Mr Singh will probably be allowed to pay HMRC in practice once a month or even quarterly – although he must file a return each week.

Date	Payments out	Ch. no.	Total	Employee costs
7.7	Cash for wages	231	515.00	515.00
14.7	Cash for wages	237	515.00	515.00
21.7	Cash for wages	246	515.00	515.00
28.7	Cash for wages	252	515.00	515.00
28.7	Inland Revenue	253	500.00	500.00

Figure 18.1 Entries for Hardip Singh's employees.

Figure 18.1 shows the entries made for these transactions. Payments made to the employees are entered under employee costs. The payment to HM Revenue & Customs also goes under employee costs. The total of the column for the four weeks comes to £2,560, which is the £600 weekly wage bill for four weeks, plus the £20 Employer NICs for each employee for four weeks.

Also written under the employee costs heading might be pension contributions made on behalf of employees, if a pension scheme is in place. Even if there are no PAYE or NICs due, perhaps because employees only worked a few hours and thus earned too little for tax to apply, wages paid should still be included in employee costs. Grace Morris, for example, includes not only the pay for a part-time worker but also the pay for children with paper rounds. In the latter case they may have no PAYE or employee or employer NIC to pay as their earnings each week are too low for these to apply.

Remember this

Care must be taken, however, to include neither the NICs nor income tax paid for the proprietor under the 'Employee costs' analysis heading. The proprietor is not an employee, and therefore his or her income tax and NICs are not an expense of the business. They are personal expenses. They belong, as has been noted earlier in the book, under 'Drawings'.

Bureaucracy of employment

While the PAYE income tax system ensures that the right amount of tax is deducted from the employee, it is the employer who has to operate the system. Calculations have to be made, payslips must be prepared, and returns submitted to HM Revenue & Customs with each payment to an employee.

Procedures for handling new employees can be time-consuming, particularly if they have lost the paperwork from their previous employment. Providing such paperwork for employees leaving is also complex and time-consuming. The PAYE system poses few difficulties for a full-time payroll department, but it may not be so easy for a small business. There are several approaches that can be considered to avoid the problem, as follows:

1 **Ensure that workers are self-employed.** Much easier said than done, but they are then responsible for their own tax affairs, and there is no need for the business owner to do anything other than pay them on receipt of invoices. However, the consequences of incorrectly categorizing a worker as self-employed can be severe, the amount paid out to them can be treated as the net payment after tax deductions, and thus the employer may have to pay the tax and NICs calculated by grossing up this net amount. Even if it were subsequently possible to recover the tax from the employee, the rights of the employer to do so are limited. Be very careful before treating a worker as self-employed, and only do so if you are sure they can be treated this way.

2 **Use a payroll bureau.** These are businesses that will, for a fee, handle the running of payrolls for other businesses, producing the necessary paperwork and informing the

employer how much to pay each employee. Bureau fees can be quite reasonable, because they will use an efficient computerized approach that few small businesses could match. Your accountant may well offer this service to their clients or will be able to recommend a bureau service to you. Do also ask other businesses you know who they use to seek out other opinions.

3 **Use an employment agency.** This is an expensive option because the agency will, of course, add its own fees. A great advantage, however, is that workers can be taken on for exactly the length of time they are needed, and without the paperwork burden imposed by the PAYE system.

Focus points

❋ Determining the employment status of people who 'work for you' is important to get right. Check it out carefully before agreeing to treat as self-employed someone who does a lot of work for you.

❋ Once you know you have employees, think about using an external agency to help manage the system to ensure you stay compliant and to minimize the work you have to do to manage this process.

❋ If you do this yourself, it is advisable to get help setting up the system you will use to help reduce the risk of making a costly mistake.

❋ Remember any wages paid to the proprietor (you) are drawings and must not be accounted for as for other employee costs.

❋ Make sure you file your returns with HMRC as you pay employees each week (or month).

❋ You will usually pay any PAYE and NIC you have deducted either monthly or quarterly. However, like VAT money you hold if you are VAT registered, remember this is really no longer your money and you should not use it to fund the normal activity of the business or you may not have it available when it is to due to be paid to HMRC. They don't like this much!

End of year totals

In this chapter you will learn:

▶ *How to total your cashbook*
▶ *How to adjust for balances brought forward*

The information given in the previous chapters is all that is needed to keep your accounting records on a day-to-day basis. If you intend to use an accountant to complete the figures and prepare your income tax return you need only complete the calculations in this chapter, then hand the records over to the accountant. If, however, you decide to handle your own financial affairs, this chapter and the five that follow demonstrate two different methods for producing your end of year results.

The first approach is designed to produce the income and expenditure information needed to complete a tax return. For a smaller business, where the owner knows the financial position of the business and requires no extra financial information, then nothing else will be required. There is no legal requirement for a small sole trader business to produce full accounts.

However, some businesses may need to produce a full set of financial statements, with an Income Statement and a 'balance sheet', the latter showing the assets and the liabilities of the business. These accounts may be required by the bank, for example, or by a potential purchaser. They can also provide useful information to a business owner who understands how to interpret them.

While some of the calculations that have been carried out in the previous chapters are also relevant for the preparation of full financial statements, Chapter 23 starts again with the end of year totals that are explained in this chapter. It then demonstrates a different way of dealing with them in order to produce what is known in accountancy jargon as a 'trial balance'. Chapter 24 explains how to use the trial balance to produce a full Income Statement and balance sheet.

The case study that will be used for the first approach is Ben Martin: his is typically the sort of business that may not need any more detail about its financial performance than the profit figure on which income tax is due. The example for the second approach is that of Grace Morris's shop, because when her business is eventually sold, a purchaser will want to see the past few years' accounts. Although it does not apply in Grace

Morris' case, such businesses are often financed by bank borrowings, and the bank might insist on seeing full accounts with both a profit and loss account, and a balance sheet. Grace's business is therefore a good example of a business that may be advised to produce full accounts, even if not strictly needed in reality for tax purposes.

Cashbook totals

After ruling off and totalling the figures for the last month of the business year, March in this case, the final year end totals must be produced. The next page in the cashbook should be headed up as 'Year ended 31 March 201X – Summary'. Enter the usual headings at the top of the analysis columns.

In the wide column in which the details of cheque payments are normally entered, write the months of the trading year, one on each line. Starting with April, copy the totals from each month's cashbook page onto this summary, so each line summarizes the totals for that month. Remember to include the blank columns to the right of the totals for both payments and receipts, which you used in the analysis to bring forward the balances from the previous month. It is easy to make mistakes when copying the figures out, so always double check that you have the right figure in the right place. To confirm this, check that the totals are still in balance.

Next add up each of the columns again, in order to get to the annual totals. In exactly the same way as the monthly totals, the analysis columns for payments must add up to the same figure as the 'Payments total' column, and the analysis columns for the receipts must add up to the same as its 'Total' column. If things do not add up in this way, check again that the figures have been transferred correctly, then use the same techniques as explained in Chapter 16 to find where the error lies.

EXAMPLE

Figure 19.1 shows the year end summary for Ben Martin, on the payments side of the analysis book. Columns which he did not use have been omitted.

Month	Total		Cost of sales	Admin.	Motor	Travel/ Subs.	Advertising	Drawings
April	1,297.26		143.80	23.46	350.00		140.00	640.00
May	1,202.79		213.45		430.34	34.00		525.00
June	1,138.54		123.54	12.00	350.00			653.00
July	2,177.01		134.29	45.23	654.23		54.00	1,289.26
August	1,190.89		210.89		385.00			595.00
September	1,191.53		145.29	16.24	350.00			680.00
October	1,744.41		134.93		723.94		265.54	620.00
November	1,367.26		218.82		382.23	68.21		698.00
December	1,374.81		268.23	22.58	350.00			734.00
January	2,138.32		187.20		480.00	25.20	120.00	1,325.92
February	1,321.46		162.00	76.23	541.23			542.00
March	1,134.28		134.28		350.00			650.00
Total	17,278.56		2,076.72	195.74	5,346.97	127.41	579.54	8,952.18

Figure 19.1 Ben Martin's payments year end summary.

He was always in credit with the bank, and so there are no entries in the blank column to the right of the total. The figure at the bottom of the 'Total' column shows that payments made in the year totalled £17,278.56, and the analysis columns that follow show what the money was spent on. A total of £8,952.18 was, in fact, not spent on business items at all, it was his drawings figure for the year.

Adjustment for balances brought forward

You may well find that the figure showing in one or both totals columns looks rather high. The reason for this is that the totals include the balances brought forward each month on the business bank account. If during the year the business fluctuated between a credit bank balance and an overdraft, both payments and receipts totals will be overstated.

Eliminate all of these monthly brought forward balances. Whatever figure appears in either (or both) of the columns totalling the brought forward balances, write it in the same column on the line underneath, but in brackets, and also write it underneath the 'Total' column in brackets. Then subtract it from the figure above. When you subtract this figure from itself there will be nothing left in the 'Brought forward' column. The 'Total' column will also be reduced by the same amount. As a result the figures will still balance. Add the figures in the analysis columns, and now that there is nothing in the 'Brought forward' column the total must be equal to the new figure in the 'Total' column.

EXAMPLE

This can be seen in Figure 19.2, showing the receipts side of the year end summary for Ben Martin. The 'Total' column adds up to £53,513.74, but this figure is meaningless. All of the brought forward bank balances (of about £3,000 each month) have been included within it. These add up to £34,622.60. This figure must be eliminated from the total to arrive at the true amount that has been paid into the account, namely £18,891.14.

	Total	Brought fwd.	Income	Cap. Int.
April	4,060.90	2,496.92	1,563.98	
May	4,312.87	2,763.64	1,349.23	200.00
June	4,239.20	2,710.08	1,529.12	
July	4,587.89	3,100.66	1,487.23	
August	3,564.00	2,410.88	1,029.12	124.00
September	4,118.26	2,373.11	1,745.15	
October	4,551.97	2,926.73	1,625.24	
November	4,304.85	2,807.56	1,497.29	
December	4,987.71	2,937.59	2,025.12	25.00
January	5,306.19	3,612.90	1,693.29	
February	4,636.12	3,167.87	1,468.25	
March	4,843.78	3,314.66	1,529.12	
Total	53,513.74	34,622.60	18,542.14	349.00
	(34,622.60)	(34,622.60)		
	18,891.14			

Figure 19.2 Ben Martin's receipts year end summary.

Further adjustments

To arrive at the information needed to enter into the tax return, certain adjustments need to be made before the totals figures shown above can be used. These are covered in the next two chapters.

Focus points

* Prepare a new page in your cashbook to show all of the year's monthly totals.
* Total these up and then perform a cross-check to arrive at the real amount that has been paid into the account during the year.
* Eliminate bank balances brought forward from the totals to arrive at the real amount that has been paid into the account during the year.
* This sum may need some adjustments to it before it is the correct one to go into the tax return as your income for the year. The next chapter discusses these adjustments.

Adjustments for payments

In this chapter you will learn:

- ▶ *How to calculate what you really earned in a year*
- ▶ *How to adjust for cost of sales*
- ▶ *How to record your adjustments*

General principles

The totals figures calculated in Chapter 19 showed how much money was spent during the year and how much money was received. The difference between the two is not necessarily the profit (or loss) for the year.

For example, suppose Mr Dylan bought 100 CDs for £5 each. He sold them all during the month for £10 each. His income and expenditure figures show purchases totalling £500 and sales of £1,000. Now suppose Mr John purchased 200 CDs for £5 each. He sold 100 of them during the month for £10 each. His income and expenditure figures show purchases of £1,000 and sales of £1,000.

Would it be correct to say Mr Dylan made £500 profit in the month whereas Mr John merely broke even? Mr John sold as many CDs as Mr Dylan, and made the same amount of profit on each one. The difference is that Mr John still had some left over to sell in the future. He had some 'closing inventory' remaining at the end of the month.

A similar problem can arise for bills received but not yet accounted for. For example, Mr John might have been invoiced for his 200 CDs but not yet paid the bill. If he sold 100 of them his books would show receipts totalling £1,000 but no payments. It would be wrong to state that he had made £1,000 profit simply because he had not paid for the CDs which he had sold.

Adjusting for these timing differences is necessary to move from a simplistic cash receipts and payments basis to what is known as the earnings (or what accountants call the 'accruals') basis.

Remember this

Although it is allowable for small businesses to prepare accounts for tax purposes on the simple receipts minus payments basis (so-called 'cash basis' for tax accounts) most business will want to make adjustments laid out in this chapter to arrive at an adjusted profit (or loss) amount, and so the details laid out in this chapter will be important for all businesses.

Cost of sales

To reach an accurate cost of sales figure, a physical count of inventory (sometimes called 'stock' in the UK) is needed to determine how much remains unsold at the end of the year. This closing inventory can then be valued at its original cost, or, if it has fallen in value since it was purchased, at the value that it could now be sold for. This means that inventory will be valued at cost unless it could now be sold only at a loss.

A manufacturing business could have three different types of inventory: raw materials, uncompleted manufacturing work in progress and finally the finished goods themselves. Each type must be valued. For raw materials the principles are straightforward, but when valuing work in progress and finished goods at 'cost' an allowance must be made not just for the raw materials used, but also for the wages, heat, light, etc. that have gone into the manufacturing process.

Service businesses do not have inventory, but may have carried out work which has not yet been billed to the customer. This is also accounted for as work in progress. We will review how to deal with this in the next chapter.

Other adjustments

The other year end adjustments needed are generally easier to calculate. At the end of the year write 'unpaid at year end' on the face of each invoice in the filing system that is still above the divider card as not yet paid. Then list these unpaid bills and total them up under each respective category of expenditure. Include the VAT-exclusive figure only if you are VAT-registered, since the VAT element will be reclaimable anyway in due course. If you are not VAT-registered, include the full amount.

Recording the adjustments

The inventory valuation and the expense category totals for the unpaid bills now need to be entered under the payments side of the year end summary, a couple of lines below the totals, and any adjustments made following guidance in the last chapter.

In the details column write 'Inventory at year end' and write the total figure for inventory under the 'Cost of sales' column. Put brackets round it, as it is to be deducted in order to reduce the cost of sales in the year by the value of inventory remaining unsold at the year end.

If this is not the first year of trading then the closing inventory figure from the end of the previous year must now be added to this year's cost of sales figure. On the next line of the summary write 'Inventory at start of year' and write it in under 'Cost of sales'. The total under the 'Cost of sales' column will now show the true 'Cost of sales' for the year.

A similar process is needed to deal with the unpaid purchase invoices. On the next line, write 'Accounts payable at year end'. Accounts payable (sometimes called creditors) are suppliers who are owed money by the business. Calculate the totals under the appropriate headings. These are added to the totals already paid in the year, because they are costs that have been incurred in the year even though the invoices themselves have not yet been paid. On the next line (again, unless this is the first set of accounts for the business where you won't have any), write 'Accounts payable at start of year' and fill in the figures from the previous year end, using brackets as they are to be deducted. Complete the totals to arrive at the true costs under each heading on a full accruals basis.

Remember this

Keep safe the working sheets showing details of the adjustments; one method is to staple them into the analysed cashbook on the page after the annual summary. Alternatively, file the working sheets in the same box file as the used cheque stubs and paying-in slips.

EXAMPLE

Ben Martin does not have any inventory, so there is no inventory adjustment needed in his accounts. (You will see an adjustment for inventory in subsequent chapters when Grace Morris prepares her year end figures.)

Mr Martin's cost of sales figure shows his total payment in the year for fuel, mainly reflecting the bills he pays from his fuel card at the beginning of each month. This payment is the cost of fuel purchased in the previous month, so there is, therefore, an unpaid bill outstanding at the year end that must be accounted for. At the year end the unpaid bill totalled £155.26, although conversely a bill for £143.80 paid in the first month of the latest year related to the previous year. In Figure 20.1 these are adjusted for. There is also a bill outstanding at the year end totalling £68 for repairs to the taxi, and this will also be included as accounts payable. There were no other accounts payable at the start of the year, and so on a full accruals basis of accounting the cost of sales figure becomes £2,088.18 and motor expenses total £5,414.97. No other adjustments are needed.

Possible adjustments

In theory, a number of other possible adjustments could be made to Ben Martin's accounts. For example, some of the advertising bills paid towards the end of year might relate to advertisements that still have time to run after his year end. He will also receive the business telephone bill in a month's time; some call costs on the bill will relate to the previous two months. Adjustments should be made for such items where they are a 'material' amount, that is to say one which is quite large relative to the size of the business's activities. It is impossible to be precise as judgement is involved here, but no adjustment would normally be made for an item costing (say) 55 pence or £36.40 perhaps, but one would definitely be made for an adjustment of (say) £100. Note also that there should be consistency in the way that expenses are treated from year to year, and HM Revenue & Customs will probably become upset if they find that someone has deliberately tried to bring in bills that relate to a period after the year end date.

	Total	Cost of sales	Admin.	Motor	Travel/ Subs.	Advertising	Drawings
	17,278.56	2,076.72	195.74	5,346.97	127.41	579.54	8,952.18
Accounts payable at y/e		155.26		68.00			
Accounts payable at start of year		(143.80)					
TOTAL		2,088.18		5,414.97			

Figure 20.1 Ben Martin's adjustments for payments.

Focus points

To make your end of year totals acceptable for most purposes like tax, you will need to make adjustments for:

* inventory
* accounts payable
* other major (i.e. materials) items.

Not all businesses have to do this – particularly if you are operating on a cash basis for producing your tax accounts – however most businesses are advised to work in this way.

Adjustments to receipts

In this chapter you will learn:

▶ *How to adjust your receipts*
▶ *How to calculate your debtors at the year end*
▶ *How to calculate your work in progress*

Just as for payments in the last chapter, receipts may also need to be adjusted to reflect transactions that relate to the year in question, but which are not yet in the cashbook. The most common example is work which has been billed to the customer but not yet been paid for.

Accounts receivable

Debtors are customers who owe monies to the business. Accountants use the term 'accounts receivable' to describe the debtors of a business. To calculate the year end figure, write 'unpaid at year end' on all invoices issued but not yet paid on 31 March (or whatever your year end is if not this date). Enter them on the year end summary in the same way as the adjustment for creditors in the last chapter. Add the debtors at the end of the current year, and subtract (i.e. remove from total receipts in the year) any debtors that were outstanding at the end of the previous year.

Businesses that sell on credit risk suffering bad debts, where it proves impossible to recover money owed to the business. If this occurs with one of your debts simply draw a line through the sales invoice and ignore it, do not include it in the debtors total at all. Since the debt will not have been included on the receipts side of the analysed cashbook, it is treated as if it had never arisen in the first place.

However, if some uncertainty exists about whether a bill will be paid, it is possible to make what is called a 'provision for doubtful debts'. HM Revenue & Customs will only allow a tax deduction for doubtful debts if they are 'specific', that is related to a particular bill. For tax purposes you are not permitted to say that, on average, you find 5% of your debts go bad and you are therefore going to make a 5% provision against all monies owed to the business at the year end. For a bad debt provision to be tax allowable you have to be able to say that you expect a particular debt to go bad for a specific reason and make a specific provision against that debt.

Note full background details on the year end accounts receivable sheet for any amount that you know is already a bad debt, and any doubtful amounts that you think may become bad debts. These invoices can be excluded from the year end accounts receivable balance that has to be added to the receipts in the year as above.

> ## Remember this
>
> If, despite expectations, a 'doubtful' balance is nevertheless collected in the following year, it will be written into the receipts side of the cashbook in the normal way during that year and thus will automatically be included in the accounts in the following year.

Work in progress

The other adjustment that may be needed is for work in progress. The difficulty for service-based businesses is typically that clients are billed only when work is complete, whereas at the year end some work will still be in progress. However, if some of the costs of carrying out the work have been incurred, it is correct that this work in progress should be valued at cost and added to the sales for the year.

From a practical point of view, if the business consists of providing only the proprietor's own skills and labour, with no other direct costs for particular jobs nor costs of employing staff to do any of the work, the adjustment for unfinished work in progress is ignored. The proprietor's own time and effort is not treated as a cost to the business for this purpose.

If you are in any doubt about the need to make a work in progress adjustment, ask for advice from a qualified accountant or from HM Revenue & Customs.

The entry is made in the normal way: simply add the value of work in progress at the end of the current year to receipts, and subtract any work in progress at the end of the previous year.

EXAMPLE

In his particular business, Ben Martin does not normally issue sales invoices, but he does have a debtor at the end of the year. The work that he did for Cab-U-Like during March this year will not be paid to him until April, and amounts to £142. Similarly, the work he did in March last year was only received by him in April of this accounting year. He included this amount, £126, in the previous year's accounts, and so must exclude it this year or it will have been counted (and taxed!) twice. He therefore adds £142 and subtracts £126 from the income figure as shown in Figure 21.1.

	Total		Income	Cap. Int.
Total	18,891.14		18,542.14	349.00
Debtors at y/e			142.00	
Debtors at start of year			(126.00)	
TOTAL			18,558.14	

Figure 21.1 Ben Martin's adjustment to receipts.

Focus points

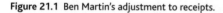

* Income totals on your receipts page must be adjusted at the year end for any debts owed to you at that point.
* If you made a similar adjustment at the end of last year, make sure you deduct that now to prevent it being accidentally counted as income twice.
* Don't include any bad debts in these adjustments.

Transfer to tax return

In this chapter you will learn:

- ▶ *The format of the self-assessment tax return*
- ▶ *How to complete your tax return*

Self-assessment tax return

Personal tax returns in the UK are completed and submitted under the self-assessment system. For business income, accounts and a tax computation are not submitted to HM Revenue & Customs; a special schedule (section) in the self-assessment form is completed instead.

It is only necessary to complete the boxes on this schedule. If business accounts, more formally called financial statements, are prepared, then balance sheet details can also be entered on the tax return form. For smaller businesses, however, there is no requirement to do so.

Indeed, for businesses with a turnover of less than the VAT registration threshold a year, the return of business income can be reduced to a three-line entry – income, total expenses, and the difference between the two as a profit or loss.

This chapter does not explain how to complete the self-assessment tax return in detail; that is beyond the scope of this book. It does explain where the figures as calculated for business income and expenditure should be entered on the form.

Finally, note that it is possible to complete and submit self-assessment tax returns for individual proprietors and for business partnerships on the internet. In fact, if you are doing your return yourself this is by far the easiest way for most people to do it. Visit HM Revenue & Customs website (www.hmrc.gov.uk) for further information.

Remember this

Check with your accountant (or local HMRC Office if you don't have one) exactly when you should complete a tax return, as failing to do this on time will cost you a penalty that rises quite quickly the longer the return is late.

Income and expenditure schedule

The tax return has a section headed 'Income and expenses' in the self-employment pages. This has a box for business income, then two parallel columns of boxes for the expense headings. The column on the right-hand side is where the figures calculated in the last few chapters should be entered. The column on the left-hand side is for disallowable expenses. Many of these were never entered into the book-keeping system described in this book; you will see in the example below that Ben Martin has to adjust for the private use element of vehicle costs.

EXAMPLE

Figure 22.1 shows the boxes as completed by Ben Martin; the layout of the self-assessment return varies slightly from year to year but you should be able to identify these boxes clearly. Most figures can be traced back to the year end summary as amended, but there are some changes.

1 Ben Martin keeps a record of vehicle mileage, separating business from private mileage. From this he calculates that 5% of total mileage is private. He therefore calculates 5% of fuel costs shown under 'Cost of sales', and 5% of the motor costs, and writes these disallowed figures in the 'disallowable' boxes.

2 He uses his home relatively little for business purposes, but nevertheless it is where he garages the cab and works on it, and where he maintains his accounting records. He is, therefore, entitled to include part of his home expenses as a tax deductible item in the accounts. Rather than go into a complicated calculation, he estimates this cost as £5 per week and adds a total of (£5 × 52 weeks) to the cost figure for premises costs. (An estimate is ok as long as it is reasonable – you can check this by asking others in the same circumstances as you are or by seeking the advice of an accountant.)

3 He pays his teenage son £3 most weeks to clean the vehicle. It is, therefore, possible for him to include the total of £141 paid in this way under employee costs.

Most entries are really quite straightforward, and can be completed by following the guidance on the HM Revenue & Customs website. The boxes for capital allowances need to be completed on the next page of the tax return, using figures calculated by the method set out in Chapter 9.

TRADING AND PROFESSIONAL INCOME
for the year ended 5 April 201X

Income (turnover)
6.16 £ _18 558_

- Cost of sales   6.17 £ _104_   6.33 £ _2088_

- Construction industry subcontractor costs   6.18 £   6.34 £

- Other direct costs   6.19 £   6.35 £

Gross profit/(loss) 6.36 £ _16 470_

other income/profits 6.37 £

- Employee costs   6.20 £   6.38 £ _141_

- Premises costs   6.21 £   6.39 £ _260_

- Repairs   6.22 £   6.40 £

- General administrative expenses   6.23 £   6.41 £ _195_

- Motor expenses   6.24 £ _270_   6.42 £ _5414_

- Travel and subsistence   6.25 £   6.43 £ _127_

- Advertising, promotion and entertainment   6.26 £   6.44 £ _579_

- Legal and professional costs   6.27 £   6.45 £

- Bad debts   6.28 £   6.46 £

- Interests   6.29 £   6.47 £

- Other finance charges   6.30 £   6.48 £

- Depreciation and loss/(profit) on sale   6.31 £   6.49 £

- Other expenses   6.32 £   6.50 £

Total expenses 6.51 £ _6716_

Net profit/(loss) 6.52 £ _9754_

Figure 22.1 Ben Martin's tax return.

Finally, Ben Martin uses the box for additional information to record that he has estimated his use of home expenses as £5 a week, that he has calculated his private mileage from his daily mileage log, and that no other disallowable expenses are included in his accounting records. There is no formal requirement to record this information, but it is a useful habit to record details of anything that the tax inspector might later query.

Focus points

* Doing a tax return annually is a requirement for almost all small businesses. Get advice on how and when you should do this (HMRC are actually very helpful if you ask!). It will save you significant grief later if you get into good habits with your tax affairs.
* Make sure you include all of your income and only include expenses related to your business.
* If you followed the advice earlier in the book for your cashbook column headings you will find these match those categories needed for the tax return. You may not have items under each box of course if these do not apply to your business.
* If you have a total income (called 'turnover' by accountants) of less than that year's VAT registration threshold, you don't need to complete the full listing of all your expenses and can enter it as one total, along with your income, to produce the profit (or loss) for the year.

Trial balance

In this chapter you will learn:

▶ *How to put together a basic set of accounts in a standard format*

▶ *What the jargon really means*

This chapter and the next one deal with more detailed accounting, and will allow the preparation of a set of accounts in a standard 'income statement' plus 'balance sheet' format (sometimes called a 'Statement of Financial Position'). It is not possible in this book to show more than the basic mechanics of producing accounts. This system also takes some short cuts, particularly in the calculation of some items on the balance sheet.

The firm recommendation here is to avoid putting together a full set of accounts unless you absolutely have to. In practice, the figures entered into your tax return including those for capital allowances, as explained in the previous chapters, together with an analysis of the debtors, creditors, inventory and bank balances, may well be sufficient financial management information for most smaller businesses so you won't need to produce these statements unless you want to, or someone (such as a bank if you want a loan) asks you to.

Income Statement versus Statement of Financial Position

An Income Statement and a Statement of Financial Position each provide different information about the activities and financial position of a business. An Income Statement summarizes the revenues and costs of a business over a stated period, often a year. A Statement of Financial Position shows the assets of a business, and its liabilities, at close of play on the last day of that period.

A Statement of Financial Position is sometimes called a balance sheet because it balances! It shows all assets owned by the business (vehicles, equipment, inventory, debtors and any money at the bank), less any monies owed by the business (its liabilities). The liabilities of a business include amounts owed back to the owner(s) which accountants call owner's equity or capital.

Using what is called the double-entry accounting system (as we mentioned in Chapter 1 this is a more detailed alternative accounting system that many businesses use as their activities get more complicated) there are two entries for everything: a debit entry and a credit entry. Up to this point, the system in this book has not referred to debits and credits, although all entries made in the cashbook have been entered twice, once in the 'Total' column and once in the appropriate analysis column, so there is a form of double entry being used, just not in a formal way. On the payments side of the cashbook, the entries in the 'Total' column are in effect the credit entries to the bank account, and the entries in the analysis columns are the corresponding debit entries, representing costs being paid, drawings taken, or assets acquired.

On the receipts side of the cashbook, entries in the 'Total' column are in effect the debit entries to the bank account, monies received, and the entries in the analysis columns the corresponding credit entries, items of income or capital introduced to the business.

For a VAT-registered business, the entries on the payments side are debit entries showing VAT reclaimable from HM Revenue & Customs; the entries on the receipts side are credit entries showing VAT amounts due to HM Revenue & Customs.

If this is beginning to sound confusing then you know why this is exactly the point at which many people decide either that they do not need a proper set of accounts, or that they are going to use the services of a qualified accountant to prepare one for them!

If you still want to continue to produce your own set of accounts, the bank account entries may have seemed to be the wrong way round. On your bank statement you will be used to seeing payments out shown as debits and receipts shown as credits. That is because the bank statement shows your account from the point of view of the bank. In other words, when an amount is paid in, from the bank's perspective that increases the amount of money that it is holding for (i.e. owes to) the account holder, and so it makes a credit entry. When a cheque or direct bank payment is paid out, that transaction reduces the amount owed to the account holder by the bank and therefore a debit entry is needed in the books of the bank.

Trial balance

This explanation is needed so you can understand how a trial balance is created, and what it illustrates for us in an accounting system. A trial balance is simply a listing of all debit and credit totals shown in the accounting records. After making all the adjustments shown in Chapter 19, what we are now referring to as debits and credits will balance (if all your entries are correct). 'Total payments out' is a credit figure, matched by the total debits shown by the analysis columns for payments. The total payments in/receipts figure is a debit, matched by the total of the analysis columns for receipts, which are all credit entries.

Remember this

The secret is to keep that balance by adopting one fundamental rule: for every debit entry there must be an equal and opposite credit entry (or set of credit entries sometimes), and vice versa. Always keep that statement in mind.

To draw up a trial balance, first convert the figures produced in Chapter 19 into a vertical format. Start on a new page of the cashbook, and write the headings down the wide column on the left-hand side. The first heading will be 'Bank', the others will reflect the column headings used in your cashbook. Only one VAT heading is needed, however.

Next write across the first two cash columns the word 'Cashbook', and label the first column 'Dr' (for 'debit') and label the second one 'Cr' (for 'credit'). Begin by entering the total payments figure into the 'Cr' column and the total receipts figure into the 'Dr' column, both against a heading 'Bank'. Then enter each of the analysis totals for payments made into the 'Dr' column opposite the appropriate heading, and enter the receipts analysis totals against the appropriate headings in the 'Cr' column. The only two headings which will have an entry in both 'Dr' and 'Cr' columns are 'Bank' and 'VAT' (if VAT-registered). Now add up the 'Dr' and the 'Cr' columns and check that they still balance!

Unless this is your first year of trading, head up the next two columns as 'Opening balance' and label them 'Dr' and 'Cr' again. This is where you have to enter the final balances from the previous year end balance sheet. If you don't have a balance sheet from the previous year, but this is not your first year of trading, you will need to draw one up. That is beyond the scope of this book and is perhaps a job for an accountant to help with.

By looking carefully at the previous Statement of Financial Position, it should be quite easy to see which balances are debits and which are credits, and how they balance when set off against each other. The debit balances are the assets: equipment, inventory, debtors and bank/cash. These are most of the entries at the top of the balance sheet. The credit balances are the liabilities, amounts owed to suppliers ('creditors' or 'accounts payable') and any overdraft amount owed to the bank. The main credit balance after those is likely to be right at the bottom of the Statement of Financial Position, being the figure of profit retained in the business and 'owed' by the business back to the proprietor.

Add new headings in the trial balance wide left-hand column for all of these items, except for 'Equipment' and 'Bank' which have been set up as trial balance headings already. Then enter the debit and credit balances from the previous balance sheet into the 'Opening balance' columns. Add up the two columns and check they still match.

The opening balances and the cashbook movements for the year have now been entered. To end this chapter, Figure 23.1 shows Grace Morris's trial balance; the figures used have been rounded to make things easier to follow. Chapter 24 will show you how to make other necessary adjustments in order to produce final accounts.

Remember this

If you need more information on Trial Balances, check out *Teach Yourself Book-keeping* or *Teach Yourself Basic Accounting* where you will find lots more detail and examples.

	Cashbook		Opening balance	
	Dr	Cr	Dr	Cr
Bank	93,000	85,500	6,000	
Cost of sales (purchases)	50,000			
Employee costs	4,000			
Premises costs	5,000			
Administrative	1,000			
Motor	1,000			
Advertising	500			
Finance charges	1,500			
Equipment	2,500		4,000	
Drawings	15,000			
Income (sales)		85,000		
Capital introduced		1,000		
VAT	5,000	7,000		
Inventory			3,000	
Accounts receivable			500	
Cash			100	
Accounts payable				1,000
Profit retained				12,600
Depreciation				
Profit for year				
	178,500	178,500	13,600	13,600

Figure 23.1 Grace Morris's trial balance: opening balances and cashbook movements.

Focus points

* For many small businesses producing a full set of accounts is not needed so the details of this chapter, and the next chapter can be ignored. If you use an accountant to produce accounts for you however, reading these chapters will show you what they are doing – what you are paying for!
* This method works, but is likely to go wrong at first if you do it yourself. It takes some practice to get it right.
* Only prepare a full set of accounts if you have to.
* For every debit there must be an equal and opposite credit.

Final accounts

In this chapter you will learn:

▶ *How to adjust payments*
▶ *How to complete your final accounts*

Adjusting payments

At this point please refer back to Chapters 20 and 21. The adjustments that you are about to make are the same as those described there.

The only adjustments to Accounts Payable (creditors) shown here are for cost of sales. If there are other accounts payable at the year end then other expense headings will need to be adjusted similarly.

Label the next two cash columns as 'Payments' and then mark them 'Dr' and 'Cr' respectively. The first step is the equivalent of 'adding back' the opening inventory and the opening creditors to purchases.

Make a 'Cr' entry against the inventory figure to remove the 'Dr' opening inventory balance, and then make a matching 'Dr' entry against the purchases figure to ensure that the total cost of sales figure for the year also includes all inventory already owned on the first day of the year. Next make a 'Dr' entry against the accounts payable opening balance figure to remove it, and then make a matching 'Cr' entry against the purchases line so that the purchases figure for the year correctly shows the impact of the brought forward account payable for purchases.

Now in the 'Dr' column enter the closing balance for inventory at the year end, and in the 'Cr' column enter the year end closing balance figure for accounts payable. Make matching and opposite entries against the purchases line, so that the year's purchases figure correctly reflects both year end inventory levels and also the accounts payable for purchases that exist at the year end but which have not yet been paid. Write neatly to fit in both figures. If you remain unclear about what these somewhat convoluted entries achieve, refer back to Chapter 20 to review the principles again.

Add the two columns up, and check that they balance.

A similar exercise must now be carried out for receipts. Label the next two cash columns as 'Receipts' and enter 'Dr' and 'Cr' respectively. Enter the opening balance for debtors against the heading in the 'Cr' column, and make a corresponding entry in the 'Dr' column against the sales line. Enter the year end closing balance for accounts receivable against the same heading, but in the 'Dr' column, and enter the same amount in the 'Cr' column on the sales line. Total the two columns to confirm that the entries match because the columns balance.

Figure 24.1 shows Grace Morris's entries for the 'Accounts Receivable' and 'Accounts Payable' columns – the other headings are omitted for simplicity. She had the following to adjust for:

▶ Accounts Payable were £2,000 at year end but only £1,000 at the start of the year.

▶ Accounts Receivable (for newspapers) totalled £800 at the year end, £500 at the start.

▶ Inventory £3,500 at the year end, £3,000 at the start.

▶ Depreciation charge £1,300 for the year. Depreciation is a cost entry needed to reflect the decrease in value of long-term assets such as equipment and vehicles (see below).

▶ Cash on hand £50 at the year end, £100 at the start.

Other adjustments

Head up the next two cash columns as 'Other adjustments'. As explained in Chapters 20 and 21 there are a number of matters which can be reflected in the accounts, but the key one is depreciation.

Depreciation has not been mentioned so far, partly because it is not taken into account for tax purposes and capital allowances are given instead. The idea of depreciation is that a figure should be written off as an expense each year to reflect the

	Payments		Receipts		Other adj.	
	Dr	Cr	Dr	Cr	Dr	Cr
Bank						
Cost of sales (purchases)	2,000 3,000	3,500 1,000				
Employee costs						
Premises costs						
Administrative						
Motor						
Advertising						
Finance charges						
Equipment						1,300
Drawings						
Income (sales)			500	800		50
Capital introduced						
VAT						
Inventory	3,500	3,000				
Accounts receivable			800	500		
Cash					50	
Accounts payable	1,000	2,000				
Profit retained						
Depreciation					1,300	
Profit for year						
	9,500	9,500	1,300	1,300	1,350	1,350

Figure 24.1 Payments, receipts and adjustments.

fall in value of your plant and equipment during that year. In practice many small businesses use a set formula such as 20% a year. There is no 'right' sum for this however and should reflect how long you expect to keep these assets of your business before you sell or replace them, i.e. using a 20% rate implies you expect (on average) to keep your assets for five years and then scrap them.

Enter a new heading in the left-hand column, an expense heading, called 'Depreciation expense'. Enter in the 'Dr' column of 'Other adjustments' the likely (it is almost certainly an estimate) depreciation charge for the year, and in the 'Cr' column enter the same amount against the heading for equipment cost.

Final accounts

Label the next two columns 'Profit and loss account' and the following two 'Balance sheet', using 'Dr' and 'Cr' headings as before. You are now going to total the figures across for each line, and enter the final figure in the appropriate column for either profit and loss or balance sheet. The easiest way to do this is to work on the profit and loss figures first, because these are all the headings that appeared in the analysed cashbook, but excluding bank, VAT, drawings, capital introduced and equipment purchased. There is also the new heading for the depreciation charge (i.e. expense).

All of the other headings will be totalled and the totals shown under the 'Balance sheet' columns.

Now add up each row, but look first to see whether, overall, the credits or the debits are higher. With most lines this should be quite easy because all expense lines are going to end up as debit totals, all income lines as credit totals. Assets will be debits, liabilities will be credits. For totals which are going to end up as debits, add up all the debits in that row, deduct the credits and enter the balance in the 'Dr' column of 'Profit and loss' if the item is an expense item, or put it in the 'Dr' column of 'Balance sheet' otherwise.

With totals that are going to end up as credits it is the other way round: add up the credits, deduct the debits, and put the result in the 'Cr' column. You should now find that the figures for closing inventory, debtors and creditors will all be as you expect; and the year end bank balance should also be correct. If you think about the entries made this is not surprising. The system takes into account the starting bank balance, adjust for total receipts and total payments, and thus the result must (should!) be the closing balance.

The final step is to add a last new heading to the left-hand column, called 'Profit for year'. Add up the total of the 'Cr' column under 'Income Statement', then subtract all the entries in the 'Dr' column. Enter the difference in the 'Dr' column of 'Profit and loss' and the 'Cr' column of 'Statement of Financial Position'. If when you are doing this difference calculation you find that the total of the 'Dr' column exceeds that of the 'Cr' column then the business has made a loss, and the difference figure goes the other way around when writing it into the trial balance. Put a loss into the 'Cr' column of 'Income Statement' and into the 'Dr' column of 'Balance sheet'.

This process is particularly difficult to understand without actually trying it, and so at this point you may like to go back through this chapter and Chapter 23, writing up the trial balance for Grace Morris and then preparing the 'Income Statement' and 'Statement of Financial Position' columns. Figure 24.2 shows how the final four columns should look.

The last stage is to enter these figures from the trial balance columns onto a set of accounts. This is really just a matter of setting out the figures into an accepted format. Follow the example in Figure 24.3 for Grace Morris. Note that if she was overdrawn at the bank, the bank figure would appear as a credit in the 'Statement of Financial Position' columns of the trial balance, and would appear with 'Accounts payable' in the balance sheet itself.

	Income Statement		Statement of Financial Position	
	Dr	Cr	Dr	Cr
Bank			13,500	
Cost of sales (purchases)	50,500			
Employee costs	4,000			
Premises costs	5,000			
Administrative	1,000			
Motor	1,000			
Advertising	500			
Finance charges	1,500			
Equipment			5,200	
Drawings			15,000	
Income (sales)		85,350		
Capital introduced				1,000
VAT				2,000
Inventory			3,500	
Accounts receivable			800	
Cash			150	
Accounts payable				2,000
Profit retained				12,600
Depreciation	1,300			
Profit for year	20,500			20,500
	85,350	85,350	38,150	38,150

Figure 24.2 Trial balance.

Balance sheet

Fixed assets:

Equipment		5,200

Current assets:

Inventory	3,500	
Accounts receivable	800	
Bank	13,500	
Cash	150	
	17,950	

Current liabilities:

Accounts payable	2,000	
VAT	2,000	
Net current assets	4,000	
		13,950
		19,150

Represented by:

Profit retained	12,600	
Profit for year	20,550	
Capital introduced	1,000	
	34,150	
Less drawings	(15,000)	
		19,150

Figure 24.3a Final accounts for Grace Morris: balance sheet.

Income Statement		
Sales		85,350
Less: Cost of sales		(50,500)
Gross profit		34,850
Less:		
Employee costs	4,000	
Premises costs	5,000	
Administrative	1,000	
Motor	1,000	
Advertising	500	
Finance charges	1,500	
Depreciation	1,300	
		(14,300)
Net profit for the year		20,550

Figure 24.3b Final accounts for Grace Morris: profit and loss account.

Focus points

❋ Perhaps at this point you have concluded that preparing full accounts is difficult. The advice given at the beginning of Chapter 23 was not to prepare them unless you absolutely have to. You can see why now!

❋ If you need further information about drawing up final accounts, you should obtain a copy of *Teach Yourself Basic Accounting* or *Teach Yourself Book-keeping*. These books teach a traditional double-entry system of book-keeping, and once you have prepared the initial trial balance as set out in Chapter 23 of this book, the principles which it explains for drawing up accounts can be applied.

❋ If you use an accountant they will do this work for you so even if you did not use one for your regular cashbook recording, it may be worthwhile employing one just for this final stage, if you need full accounts for any reason (see Appendix 1 for hints on what to look for when choosing an accountant).

Budgeting and cash-flow forecasting

In this chapter you will learn:

▶ *How to budget for the future*
▶ *How to plan your expenditure*
▶ *How to keep your finances in check*

Thus far the accounting system in this book has been backward-looking, recording how well the business has performed in the past. Good financial control of a business should also be a forward-looking process, planning in advance how much cash or overdraft facility will be needed to cover future business needs.

Preparing a budget of future costs and forecasting business cash-flow is a helpful discipline to get into, although many small businesses don't do it. The method set out here aims to minimize the amount of work involved while still giving you a useful prediction to help you manage the financial aspects of your business.

An ideal way to prepare budgets and cash-flow forecasts is to use a computer program known as a spreadsheet. Microsoft Excel™ is one of the market leading programs, but there are many others that are similar in operation (e.g. perhaps try Open Office spreadsheet – it is freely available online). Spreadsheet programs are useful in this whole area because they allow assumptions to be changed easily in order to reveal the effects of the changes on business finances. Chapter 27 outlines computerization issues.

Budgeting

The budgeting process is an essential part of costing, which is dealt with in the next chapter. A large part of the budgeting process reflects the sorts of calculations that you may be familiar with from your own personal finances, calculating monthly outgoings and anticipating the timing of bills. These same skills apply to budgeting for a business.

At the outset, however, an important distinction between what are called 'fixed' and 'variable' costs must be understood. In the situation of Grace Morris's shop, some costs are quite fixed in amount, and can be accurately predicted in advance. These would include business rates, but also in Mrs Morris's case the shop's electricity bill, for example. Unless she changes the opening hours her electricity bill is unlikely to be much affected by the amount that she sells. Whether the shop gets one customer per hour or 20, roughly the same amount of electricity will be consumed.

On the other hand, certain costs will vary directly with the amount of sales. The most obvious is the cost of sales figure itself. If sales doubled, the cost of sales would probably double also. For Grace Morris, purchases are likely to be the main variable cost as she would need to go to the Cash and Carry more often.

For Hardip Singh's building business, materials costs will vary with sales, so too will labour costs and probably hire costs for machinery.

Layout of a budget

The distinction between variable and fixed costs is clearly visible in the layout of an expenses budget. Figure 25.1 shows Hardip Singh's budget for the three months ending in October. He finds it easiest to use a three-monthly budget based on his

	Budget	Actual	Variance	Reason
Sales	25,000	22,000	–3,000	Budget too optimistic
Direct expenses				
Materials	6,000	6,000	–	
Labour	6,000	5,500	–500	
Other direct costs	500	500	–	
Gross profit	12,500 (50%)	12,000 (54%)	–2,500 –5%	Paid for materials and labour R. Henderson, not billed
Other expenses				
Motor	500	490	–10	
Admin.	1,500	1,700	+ 200	Stationery
Advertising	500	510	+10	
Net profit	10,000	7,300	–2,700	

Figure 25.1 Hardip Singh's three-monthly report: budget versus actual.

VAT quarters, and since as he has to prepare figures for the VAT return it does not take much longer to fill in the actual outcome of the three months on his budget sheet.

The first heading is 'Sales'. This figure is the sales invoiced during the period, not the amounts actually received from customers. For Hardip Singh this is found by simply totalling the invoices in his book that remain outstanding at the end of the three months, adding this total to the figure entered on the VAT return for income actually received, and subtracting the invoices that had been outstanding at the end of the previous quarter. It is necessary to reflect sales invoiced because direct costs for his business are likely to reflect the work actually done during the quarter, not just the work that customers have paid for.

'Materials', 'Labour' and 'Other' direct costs (hire of machinery in this case) are the first expense headings below the sales line. These variable costs are totalled and then deducted from sales to give a figure known as the 'gross profit'.

It is difficult to predict what the gross profit amount will be, but what should not change very much from one period to the next is the gross profit percentage. This figure is calculated by dividing gross profit by the sales and multiplying the result by 100. Since by definition direct expenses vary directly with sales, the percentage should not vary much between trading periods. It is for precisely this reason that HM Revenue & Customs looks closely at variations in gross profit levels as one of its core checks of your accounts when you file a tax return, comparing movements from one year to the next and comparing a particular business's gross profitability with industry averages.

Following the gross profit line come the expenses which do not vary directly with sales activity. These costs may not be 'fixed' in absolute terms but will vary with sales activity a great deal less than 'variable' costs will. The main concern with fixed costs is how accurately they can be forecast.

In the first column of figures Hardip Singh entered his budget for the period. He estimated that he would achieve sales of £25,000, and that the direct expenses would be running at 50%

of that. After that come the various fixed expenses, to give a budgeted profit of £10,000 for the quarter.

The second column shows the actual outcome. Sales were lower than expected, and the gross profit percentage was also lower. Most of the fixed expenses were more or less in line with what had been expected, although general administrative expenses were higher.

The point of preparing a budget is then to use it to analyse actual performance. The next two columns do this. The first shows the difference between the budget and the actual outcome, and the last column records an explanation for the variations.

The shortfall in Hardip Singh's sales performance was identified as an over-optimistic budget; it might equally have been an unexpected downturn in business activity, or perhaps a period when Mr Singh was unexpectedly absent from the business. However, the sales shortfall does not explain why the gross profit percentage is lower than normal. Looking at his records Mr Singh identifies the reason: he had already paid for some materials and labour for a job that has not been finished and therefore not billed. There is also an explanation for the increased general administrative costs, in that new stationery was needed for which he had forgotten to budget.

The sales shortfall may therefore be the main cause for concern, and if necessary he should consider ways of generating more business.

Remember this

This process of analysing your business via a budget is a very useful way of staying in touch with exactly what is happening and helps you keep in mind the big picture.

Cash-flow forecasting

After preparing a budget setting out anticipated future sales revenues and costs, cash-flow forecasting can be useful in estimating cash needs of the business over the coming months. Cash-flow forecasting should be done monthly, perhaps with a rolling three-month forecast updated each month. Essentially, cash-flow forecasting is an exercise in predicting what the cashbook totals will be.

EXAMPLE

Mr Singh is going to meet the bank manager because he wants to take on a major job over the next four months. Payment will be on what is called a 'cost plus' basis, that is to say costs will be reimbursed in full plus a mark-up to cover Mr Singh's own time and to give a profit margin. In this particular case there will be a 20% mark-up on costs. At £8,000 each month costs will be substantial: £3,000 for materials and £5,000 for labour. He can delay paying for materials until a month after the purchase invoice is received, but he must pay for labour each week. He will be paid for materials two months in arrears, but the rest of his invoices will not be paid until two months after the work is completed.

Figure 25.2 shows the cash-flow forecast for this particular job, but normally a cash-flow would be put together for the whole of the business, being built up from individual jobs.

Month	1	2	3	4	5	6
Income	–	–	3,000	3,000	3,000	29,400
Outgoings:						
Materials	–	(3,000)	(3,000)	(3,000)	(3,000)	–
Labour	(5,000)	(5,000)	(5,000)	(5,000)	–	–
Balance b/f	–	(5,000)	(13,000)	(18,000)	(23,000)	(23,000)
Balance c/f	(5,000)	(13,000)	(18,000)	(23,000)	(23,000)	6,400

Figure 25.2 Hardip Singh's cash-flow forecast.

In the first month the only payment anticipated is the £5,000 for labour costs, since Mr Singh does not expect to have paid the first materials bill yet. This means that by the end of month 1 the overdraft would rise to £5,000 to finance the work. In month 2 he still receives nothing, but pays out £8,000: a second month's £5,000 for labour and the first month's bill for materials. The overdraft has thus gone up to a total of £13,000 by the end of month 2.

In both months 3 and 4 he should receive £3,000 from the customer, being his materials costs from months 1 and 2, but also pays out for the materials bought in months 2 and 3. Mr Singh also pays his workforce as before, and so by the end of month 4 the overdraft is up to £23,000 in total.

By month 5 the work is finished so he does not have to pay any further labour costs, but he does pay the materials bill for month 4 and also receives the reimbursement for his materials costs from month 3. Finally, in month 6 Hardip receives the payment covering month 4's materials, the £20,000 he had paid for labour over the entire job, and the 20% profit margin, leaving, at last, a cash surplus.

This is, of course, only a forecast and things may actually turn out differently. However, on the basis of the cash-flow figures Mr Singh can approach his bank and request an increase in his overdraft facility of £25,000 for seven months. The bank is likely to want to see this computation so they can understand where the request for this particular sum comes from, and to understand how Mr Singh proposes to repay any overdraft he receives.

Note that despite the forecast showing a maximum overdraft requirement of £23,000, he is wise to seek a slightly larger amount to cover any unforeseen costs, and possible late payment by the customer.

Focus points

* Budgets allow you to compare your expected results with the actual results to identify problem areas.

* Budgets require sales and purchases figures, not just cash received and paid.

* Cash-flow forecasting uses best estimates of the timing of cash coming in and cash going out.

* Cash-flow forecasting is based upon budgets, but with adjustments for timing differences.

* If you wish to make use of an overdraft a bank is likely to ask you to produce a cash-flow forecast and a budget to help them understand your business, and to give them confidence you are in good control of your business.

* Even if you are funding any short-term lack of cash yourself, it is still a good idea to make these forecasts explicitly. Not doing so is a key reason small businesses get into financial trouble – so don't be one of them!

Costing and pricing

In this chapter you will learn:

▶ *How to price your goods or services*
▶ *The dangers of underpricing*
▶ *How to remain competitive while still making money*

Costing is an entire subject in itself, and there are many different methods for allocating costs to business activities. In a small business, however, things can be relatively straightforward, and this chapter is designed to give an introduction to the subject from a smaller business perspective.

Costing is linked to the rather tricky area of pricing. There is a well-known tendency for small businesses to under-price, competing solely by being cheaper than the competition. Research suggests that this can lead to business failure, and that a proper understanding of what customers are looking for, and of how to price for it, partly based on costs, can help a fledgling business to survive and thrive.

Remember this

A key point to note is that costing is a science, based upon assumptions and calculations; pricing uses that information, but is much more subjective than that. Some would say that pricing is actually more of an art form.

Costing

Business owners sometimes forget to include the cost of their own time. If you run a business you expect to get something out of it and so don't ignore the value of your own efforts. In a service industry, the time spent by staff is likely to be the most important element of costs. Ensure that it is properly recorded, using timesheets to record where staff have spent the time that they have been paid for.

Pricing

In order to understand how to price items, the concept of fixed and variable costs is again helpful; refer back to Chapter 25 for a refresher. If an item is sold for more than its variable cost, a gross profit will result. If Grace Morris sells an item for more than she paid for it she will have made a gross profit. However, if she sold every item at just one penny more than she paid for it, she would soon go out of business because the total gross profit would not be sufficient to cover business overheads. She would make a net loss.

In order to set price levels, Grace Morris could instead start by establishing an overall mark-up that she needs to achieve. To begin with she must estimate the cost of the inventory that will sell in a week, say £2,000. Next she estimates total overhead costs for the year, and divides that by 52 to arrive at a weekly average figure. That might come to £200. Finally she adds the cost of her own time at (say) £300 a week. Thus every £2,000 of inventory purchased must be sold on average for at least £2,500 in order to cover the shop's overheads and to make a profit. She therefore needs to mark up her goods by at least 25% to achieve this.

What if Mrs Morris were to be approached by a local campsite which runs a small on-site shop? In the past they had bought their own goods from the Cash and Carry, but that is proving too time-consuming. Would she be prepared to sell £500 of goods a week to them at a discount of 10% from her normal prices?

The key question is whether this is additional business, over and above the business that Mrs Morris's shop is already getting? She would be supplying goods for £450 that would normally sell for £500. The goods will have cost only £400, overheads will not alter, so she would make an additional £50 in profit each week, assuming campers would not have come into her shop anyway.

Pricing is about the need to make enough sales at a sufficiently high mark-up to cover overheads, together with exploiting any opportunities for making genuinely additional sales at anything over the 'marginal' cost of the goods or services being sold. Marginal cost means variable cost, normally the direct costs of getting items for sale into their present location and condition.

Sometimes there may be little discretion over price, for example, where there is a set market rate. Calculations can then be carried out the other way round. Say, for example, Grace Morris knew that she was going to achieve a mark-up of only 20%, because of fierce price competition with other shops. She still has to make an extra £500 a week to cover her overheads and the cost of her own time. If this is to be only 20% of the cost of the goods she will sell, it follows that she must sell £2,500 of goods each week (on average) in order to do so. If she does not achieve this level of sales then profits, the reward for her own time, will suffer. In addition she can look at changing the mix of goods on offer in the shop in order to achieve a higher gross profit, and she can always look for ways to cut overheads.

Business owners need to use all approaches flexibly. It is not possible simply to set prices without reference to those of competitors, but competing solely on price will lead to a need to generate high sales volumes in order to make a profit after overheads. Pricing is an art as much as a science, but an understanding of the basic principles can allow much better business decisions based on more than just guesswork.

Remember this

Remember always that you do not need to make absolutely correct decisions all of the time, you simply need to be better than the competition!

Focus points

✵ Costing correctly is an important part of running a successful business.
✵ Don't forget to include your own time as a cost.
✵ Operating on a fixed mark-up basis might be a good way to calculate your prices, but understanding your costs better will help you determine if a job priced at lower than your usual mark-up is worth taking on.

Computerization

In this chapter you will learn:

- ▶ *The principles of spreadsheets*
- ▶ *How to choose an accounting package*
- ▶ *How to back up your system*

A computer can certainly help in minimizing some of the drudgery when preparing accounting records or undertaking financial management tasks like creating budgets or cashflows. Using the methods set out in the rest of this book, a spreadsheet can usually be used instead of a handwritten analysed cashbook, and the spreadsheet will handle the calculations quickly and accurately, speeding up the time it takes to get month and year end totals for example. Please do not expect a computer program to do the thinking for you; that bit will always be down to you and so the principles we have discussed throughout the book will continue to be critical to getting your accounts right even if you do use a computer to help.

You also need to be careful to put into the computer sensible numbers so that the outcome be useful to you. Take care over thinking what numbers you enter into the spreadsheet just as you would when doing this by hand.

Spreadsheets

An analysed cashbook is really nothing more than a series of manual spreadsheets, and setting one up using a spreadsheet program will save time in the long run and reduce the possibility of errors. The arithmetic computations involved are simple. If you have a high-end office suite such as Open Office or Microsoft Office™, and you are not familiar with the spreadsheet package, you will probably find that you can set up a table in a word processor program which will do the job just as well and will be less daunting to use. On the other hand, if you can get to grips with the spreadsheet package, you will be able to get much better analysis data from it, including charts and graphs that you may find much easier to read than tables of figures on their own. The time invested to get to grips with your spreadsheet program is therefore probably time well spent.

Remember this

The simplest approach is to draw up a standard format spreadsheet including all the headings referred to in this book, which is then saved and re-loaded under a different name each month. Remember to set the options in the spreadsheet for currency format (two fixed decimal places) and for brackets to be used to show negatives.

A handy way of checking that the rows of analysis have been correctly entered is to put a check formula at the end of the row, which adds up the individual entries and then subtracts the total from the existing total in the spreadsheet row. The result should equal zero otherwise an error has occurred. The same approach can be used to cross-check totals at the bottom of the sheet.

Accounting packages

For a smaller business, spending money on more complex accounting packages may not be necessary. Look for programs sold as small business accounting packages (e.g. the market leader is Sage Instant) which will cope very well with your basic accounting needs until your business gets large enough to need a specialist accounting professional to work with you. With the understanding gained from this book there will be a way of entering most transactions to ensure that they are accurately recorded. If you are going to use a simple accounting package do make sure that it can handle VAT if you are (or are likely to become) VAT-registered.

CLOUD-BASED ACCOUNTING PACKAGES

You will also find that Cloud-based accounting packages are becoming popular. They can be an effective solution if you want your accounts to be available to you across a variety of devices (smartphones, tablets etc. as well as your PC).

Clearboooks (http://www.clearbooks.co.uk) is a good example. This package can also include integrated HR and payroll tools. The other advantage of Cloud-based solutions is you just pay a small monthly fee to 'rent' the software, you don't need to pay upfront to buy it. If you use an accountant check with them which Cloud-based solution they recommend as this will make their life easier if you use the one they prefer.

Other Cloud-based packages you may want to look at include:

▶ QuickBooks Online (QBO) (http://www.intuit.co.uk/quickbooks)

▶ Zero (http://www.xero.com)

- Freeagent/Iris Openbooks (http://www.freeagent.com)

- Sage One Accounts (http://www.sage.co.uk)

Other options also exist and new products come to this new market regularly. Different products appear to fit different needs better. Most have a trial or demo capability so you can test them out first before you commit to using them.

Back-ups

An advantage of manually keeping a cashbook is that it is far harder to lose. Electronic information is easy to delete by accident. Always keep a separate back-up copy of the accounting records on a computer, and ensure that this is updated regularly. It is also wise to print out the records each month so that you also have a paper copy. (If you go for a Cloud-based solution this is done automatically for you – another advantage of these solutions.)

Remember this

Speak to the person who will prepare your final accounts (if you don't plan to do this yourself) about how best to set up the computerized parts of your accounting systems. They will most likely have lots of experience of others who have done this and will be able to advise you on how best to achieve what you need.

Internet

An email account is useful as a further means of contacting suppliers and for customers to contact you (and vice versa). In some businesses, even if very small, this may actually be essential. However, this may not always be the case if you are a local business with a 'word of mouth' sales strategy.

If you don't know how to set up an email account then asking a good IT professional would be the best way forward. This doesn't have to be expensive to set up and operate, nor technically complicated, and you can often get a more than adequate email service from the company that supplies internet access at your home or business premises. Alternatively, the free email services that many people use for private emails (e.g. Google Mail and

Hotmail are just two examples) may also be more than adequate to get you started with using email for your business.

Once you have an email account this can be a good way of sending and receiving any paperwork associated with effectively managing your accounting system (invoices, credit notes and so on). This will not only save you postage and speed up delivery of these documents, but also provides a good tool for prompting anyone who owes you money to pay up!

As your business grows it may also prove useful, or essential in some types of business, to get a website. Your internet provider may again be able to help you with this very cheaply and this is perhaps the best place to start. However, as you get a better idea of how you want to use your website to sell your products or services then many different options for creating a very impressive web 'presence' can now be found fairly easily and cheaply. A website can be an excellent way of generating business, advertising your prices and so on.

Focus points

* Spreadsheet programs can be used just like analysis books and can save you lots of time with complicated calculations. The principles explained in this book can then be used in just the same way.
* Accounting packages may not be needed for your very small business initially but may prove useful as your business grows.
* Think about how the internet may be useful to you in making your accounting activities as efficient as they can be. Email is likely to be essential to you and a website may also be a useful and cost-effective way to promote your business.
* Cloud-based solutions offer a variety of benefits over other locally managed solutions. For example, they are available across a variety of devices (your smartphone, tablet and PC), you don't have to buy the software upfront but just 'rent' it on a monthly or annual basis, and you don't have to worry about back-ups as the system will do this for you as part of the service.
* Speak to your accountant, or other businesses you know, to get advice as to which solution is best for your needs. Do your research as getting this wrong will waste a lot of time.

Appendices

Appendix 1: Ten top tips for choosing an accountant

1 **Qualifications.** Ensure that you choose a qualified accountant. In the UK anyone is allowed to describe themselves as an 'accountant', the word is not currently protected by law. A Chartered Accountant will have the initials ACA or FCA after their name, a Chartered Certified Accountant will have the letters ACCA or FCCA after their name.

2 **Referrals.** Talk to your contacts and find out who they would recommend. Always remember that a slick brochure or a well-designed website may well reflect a reliable firm, but it may also simply reflect the quality of the accountant's PR firm and the size of the marketing budget.

3 **Invest time.** Meet two or three accountants, and do check in advance that the initial exploratory meeting will be at no charge.

4 **Expertise and empowerment.** Ask about their experience in dealing with your size and type of business. Can they explain accounting jargon simply and do they have a mission to help you understand the accountancy process?

5 **Contact point.** Ask who would be your main day-to-day contact. You may meet a partner with strong interpersonal and marketing skills but find that your affairs are being dealt with by a junior member of staff.

6 **Fixed fees.** Ask for a fixed annual fee quotation, in writing, to cover all of your normal business needs. Hourly rates matter, but are in fact far less important than the time taken to complete the work.

7 **Added value.** Ask what other added-value services are available if you should need them, such as handling the monthly payroll or your VAT return. You may decide that

you prefer to free up your own time to do what you are best at.

8 **Chemistry.** Is the person who would handle your affairs someone who really empathizes with your needs, and do they really understand the problems of running a smaller business?

9 **Discuss process.** Ask them about their work practices to ensure you are comfortable with what they will want from you and when, how quickly you'll get their work back, and so on. Getting all these practical aspects arranged smoothly at an early stage is critical to a good working relationship.

10 **Self-help.** Ask for suggestions about what you can do at your end to reduce your annual costs to a minimum.

Appendix 2: Jargonbuster

The following list defines key financial jargon. It is included as a brief guide within the scope of the book-keeping system described in this book.

accrual a liability that you have had the benefit of but not as yet paid for e.g. paying bills in arrears

asset *see* 'current assets' and 'fixed assets'

bank overdraft a borrowing facility, repayable on demand

bank reconciliation a procedure that reconciles the balance shown by the cashbook to the balance shown by the bank statement to check for errors in your cashbook or any missed entries that go direct to the bank account

budget an estimate of future costs and revenues, usually employed as a means of measuring actual business performance against your plans and enabling you to highlight above-budget and below-budget performance

capital funds introduced into a business by its owner, plus any profits made less any losses made

cash-flow forecast a financial forecast showing expected cash inflows and outflows over a forthcoming period

creditor a party to whom money is owed by a business (called account payable by accountants)

current assets short-term assets, including bank and cash balances, any stocks and work in progress, plus debtors and any prepayments. These are either bank or cash funds already, or items that should turn into cash within the course of the next year

current liabilities liabilities which fall due within one year, usually total creditors plus accruals

debtor a party who owes money due to a business (called account receivable by accountants)

depreciation a cost estimate of the decrease in value over a given period of a fixed asset resulting, for example, from its physical wearing out or obsolescence

double-entry book-keeping a book-keeping method that requires the use of both debit and credit entries to record each financial transaction

fixed assets assets held that have an expected life of more than one year and which are held for long-term use rather than for resale in normal trading. Buildings, vehicles, plant and machinery, and office equipment are common categories

Income statement an accounting statement showing whether a business has made a profit or incurred a loss by subtracting costs from revenues over a given period (sometimes called a profit and loss account)

liability an amount owed by a business

petty cash a small balance held in cash, available to pay for minor items of expenditure

prepayment a cost item paid for in advance of using it

Statement of financial position an accounting statement revealing the financial position of a business at a given point, by showing its assets and its liabilities and balanced by what the business 'owes' you (sometimes called a **balance sheet**)

trial balance a full listing of account headings and their balances at a given date

Appendix 3: Stationery list

This appendix sets out a 'shopping list' of stationery needed for preparing and filing accounting records in accordance with the system set out in this book.

You can find these in large stationery shops or on the internet. Initially it is probably best to go to a shop where you can look at the items to check what you need.

▶ 32 **cash column analysis book.** This is described and illustrated in Chapter 7. An alternative is a loose-leaf book, but it is then easier to mislay sheets after the year ends when they are removed.

▶ **Lever-arch file for invoices paid.** This should be a large file, the lever arch mechanism and clip to hold the papers flat are important since you will be continually opening and closing this file, and it needs to stand up to the heavy use. Don't buy a four-ring file unless you also purchase a four-ring hole punch!

▶ **Divider card.** To separate the paid and unpaid invoices.

▶ **Either: Another lever-arch file and divider card, or a duplicate invoice book.** These are sold pre-numbered with carbon sheets. Start a new one each year, so don't buy a 250-sheet book if you are only going to issue 50 or so invoices. Make sure you buy the invoices version, not the statements or orders version.

▶ **A4 paper.** To fasten till receipts, etc. to.

▶ **Box file.** Obtain one with a retaining clip to hold papers down securely and a catch to hold the lid in place when it is closed. This box will hold your cheque-book stubs, paying-in book counterfoils, invoices paid and invoices received, when the year is finished.

▶ **Calculator.** You do not need a complicated scientific or financial calculator, but a memory function and (if you are VAT-registered) a percentage button are useful. The most important thing is that it should have large enough buttons and a clear enough display for you not to make mistakes.

It may be useful to buy a calculator with a tally roll print-out, so that you can double check that you have entered all the figures. However, these are more expensive.

▶ **Stapler.** Large enough to staple through a thick wad of paper.

▶ **Treasury tags.** These are the pieces of green string with metal tags on the end used to hold together hole-punched papers. You will need long ones so that you can fasten together invoices, bank statements and so on at the end of each year before putting them into the box file.

▶ **Petty cash tin.** Not essential, since something like a biscuit tin can work equally well, but the lock may be useful.

▶ **Petty cash slips.** Again not essential, but pre-printed slips are cheap and will remind you to fill in important details.

Appendix 4: Recording sales of assets in a set of accounts

One of the more difficult things to deal with in preparing a full set of accounts is the sale of a fixed asset, such as a car or a piece of equipment. There are three ways of approaching this problem.

METHOD 1

Treat the asset disposal as a negative expense, as set out earlier in this book. This will give a set of accounts that balance, but the presentation of fixed assets on the balance sheet will not be in the normal accountancy format, nor will it give the same figure that a more conventional method would give.

METHOD 2

Keep a detailed set of records showing, for each, the acquisition cost and accumulated depreciation to date. Essentially this involves not deducting the depreciation from the cost of the assets each year, but keeping it as a running total. In the balance sheet the assets are shown at their original cost, and then the accumulated depreciation to date is deducted. When the asset is finally sold the original cost is deducted from the assets total, and the total depreciation to date charged on it is deducted from accumulated depreciation. Any resulting loss (or profit) against book value is shown as a separate item within expenses on the profit and loss account, putting it in as a negative figure if the result is a profit. Under this method the balance sheet figures for fixed assets, accumulated depreciation and the net book value arising will be as required by traditional accounting. If you decide to follow this approach you may need a book that provides more detailed guidance on traditional double-entry accounting, such as *Teach Yourself Basic Accounting* or *Teach Yourself Book-keeping*.

METHOD 3

This method involves using debits and credits. Use it only if you are confident about these terms. It can be used if you need a set of accounts that gives the same figures on your balance sheet as traditional accounting would have done, albeit with a slightly unorthodox layout. It will work best if you dispose of fixed assets only rarely, because there is quite a lot of accounting spadework involved. It gets to the same net result as method 2, and by a similar calculation, but without the need to have kept accumulated depreciation records.

Make the following adjustments to the trial balance before making the calculation for depreciation for the year. It is assumed here that the sale proceeds have already been recorded as negative expenses, as set out in Chapter 9.

1 Identify the original purchase cost of the fixed asset sold.

2 By using the annual percentage used to calculate depreciation when preparing each year's final accounts (see Chapter 19), calculate the total depreciation deducted so far from the asset. As a reminder, each depreciation percentage has been charged to the reduced balance. Thus if a computer cost £1,000 and is depreciated by 20% a year, in the first year the charge for depreciation was £200, but in the second year it was only £160, being £(1,000 – £200) × 20%.

3 Subtract the total depreciation from the original cost. The figure thus derived is the 'net book value', the 'undepreciated amount' that is in the balance sheet for the asset at the date of its disposal.

4 Compare the amount recorded as a negative expense for the money received when selling this asset: was this more than or less than the net book value? If it was more, a profit was made on the asset sale; if it was less then there was a loss.

5 If a profit was made on the sale, credit the depreciation expense account and debit the plant and machinery account with the amount. If a loss was made, the entries are to debit the depreciation expense account and credit the plant and machinery account with the loss.

Then calculate the depreciation charge for the year on the balance remaining on the plant and machinery account (as before) and prepare the final accounts. Change 'Depreciation' in the profit and loss account to 'Depreciation and profit/loss on sale'.

Note that if a profit was made on the sale, it means that effectively too much depreciation had been charged in the past; if a loss was incurred, it really means that too little had been charged for depreciation while the asset was held. The method 3 entries therefore simply reverse those over- or under-estimates of depreciation.

Index